Liverpool Everyman and Playhouse present the world première of

Intemperance

by Lizzie Nunnery

First performed on 21 September 2007 at the Everyman Theatre, Liverpool

About the Liverpool Everyman and Playhouse

As Liverpool prepares to take on the mantle of European Capital of Culture in 2008, the Everyman and Playhouse are experiencing a dramatic upsurge in creative activity. Since January 2004, we have been continually in production, creating shows which have ensured that 'Made In Liverpool' is widely recognised as a stamp of theatrical quality once again.

Around our in-house productions, we host some of the finest touring companies from around the country, to offer a rich and varied programme for the people of Liverpool and Merseyside, and for the increasing number of visitors to our city.

But there is more to these theatres than simply the work on our stages. We have a busy Literary Department, working to nurture the next generation of Liverpool Playwrights. A wide-ranging community department takes our work to all corners of the city and surrounding areas, and works in partnership with schools, colleges, youth and community groups to open up the theatre to all.

Our aim is for these theatres to be an engine for creative excellence, artistic adventure, and audience involvement; firmly rooted in our community, yet both national and international in scope and ambition.

13 Hope Street, Liverpool, L1 9BH
www.everymanplayhouse.com
Company Registration No. 3802476 Registered Charity No. 1081229

Liverpool Everyman and Playhouse would like to thanks all our current funders:

Corporate Members 7 Harrington Street Chambers, A C Robinson and Associates, Barbara McVey, Beetham Organisation, Benson Signs, Brabners Chaffe Street, Bruntwood, Chadwick Chartered Accountants, Concept Communications, Downtown Liverpool in Business, Duncan Sheard Glass, Crushed Apple Photography, DWF Solicitors, EEF NorthWest, Grant Thornton, Hope Street Hotel, Lime Pictures, Lloyds TSB Corporate Markets, Mando Group, Morgenrot Chevaliers, Radio City 96.7, Synergy Colour Printing, The Mersey Partnership, Victor Huglin Carpets.

Trusts & Foundations The PH Holt Charitable Trust, The Eleanor Rathbone Charitable Trust, The Granada Foundation, The Lynn Foundation, The Peggy Ramsay Foundation, Liverpool Culture Company, The Rex Makin Charitable Trust, The Golsoncott Foundation, The Pilkington General Fund, The Harry Pilkington Trust, The Garrick Trust, The Julia Marmor Trust, The Ernest Cook Trust, The Penny Cress Charitable Trust, Malcolm and Roger Frood in memory of Graham and Joan Frood, The Helen Hamlyn Foundation, E Alec Coleman Charitable Trust, Duchy of Lancaster Benevolent Fund, Coutts & Co. Charitable Trust, EMS Cotton Charitable Trust, Fenton Arts Trust, Kobler Trust, See A Voice, Vanderwall Trust, The Wethered Bequest.

And our growing number of individual supporters.

New Writing at the Liverpool Everyman and Playhouse

"The Everyman is back producing the next generation of Liverpool playwrights."
(The Guardian)

At the beating heart of the theatre's renaissance is our work with writers; since it is our passionate belief that an investment in new writing is an investment in our theatrical future.

Intemperance is the latest in a rich and varied slate of world, european and regional premières which has been enthusiastically received by Merseyside audiences and helped to put Liverpool's theatre back on the national map.

"The Everyman in Liverpool is living up to its name. Thanks to a new play, it is doing what theatres all over the country dream of: pulling in scores of first time theatre goers alongside loyal subscribers... blazes with energetic intelligence... this will change people's minds and in unexpected ways." (The Observer on *Unprotected*)

In just over two years, the theatres will have produced ten World Premières of plays developed and nurtured in Liverpool - most recently including *The May Queen* by Stephen Sharkey, *The Electric Hills* by Michael McLean, *The Flint Street Nativity* by Tim Firth, *The Way Home* by Chloë Moss, *Paradise Bound* by Jonathan Larkin and *Unprotected* by Esther Wilson, John Fay, Tony Green and Lizzie Nunnery, which transferred to the Edinburgh Festival where it won the Amnesty International Freedom of Expression Award.

"A remarkable renaissance." (Liverpool Daily Post)

Other highly acclaimed productions have included the European première of *Yellowman* by Dael Orlandersmith, which transferred to Hampstead Theatre and successfully toured nationally, and regional premières of Conor McPherson's *Port Authority*, Simon Block's *Chimps* and Gregory Burke's *On Tour* - a co-production with London's Royal Court Theatre.

As we prepare to celebrate European Capital of Culture in 2008, the Theatres have a variety of exciting projects in development which grow on the foundations of recent work.

"A stunning theatrical coup." (Liverpool Echo on *Unprotected*)

Around the main production programme, the theatres run a range of projects and activities to create opportunities and endeavour to support writers at every career stage.
The commissioning programme invests in the creation of new work for both the Everyman and Playhouse stages.

The Young Writer's Programme is a year-long programme working alongside experienced practitioners, which nurtures and develops exciting new voices to create a new generation of Liverpool writers. An annual new writing festival, Everyword, offers a busy and popular week of seminars, sofa talks and work-in-progress readings.

"A rare play that captures the essence of Liverpool and its people without plunging into the usual clichés." (Liverpool Daily Post on *Paradise Bound*)

For more information about the Everyman and Playhouse - including the full programme, off-stage activities such as Playwright Support, and ways in which you can support our investment in talent - visit www.everymanplayhouse.com

Credits

Cast (in alphabetical order)

Millie Sildness	**Brid Brennan**
Fergal Monahan	**Brendan Conroy**
Ruairi McLoughlin	**Matthew Dunphy**
Brynjar Sildness	**Kristofer Gummerus**
Niamh McLoughlin	**Emily Taaffe**

Company

Writer	**Lizzie Nunnery**
Director	**Gemma Bodinetz**
Designer	**Ruari Murchison**
Composer	**Conor Linehan**
Sound Designer	**Fergus O'Hare**
Lighting Designer	**Paul Keogan**
Assistant Director	**Lucy Kerbel**
Costume Supervisor	**Jacquie Davies**
Casting Director	**Ginny Schiller**
Production Manager	**Sean Pritchard**
Stage Manager	**Sarah Lewis**
Deputy Stage Manager	**Roxanne Vella**
Assistant Stage Manager	**Jo Heffernan**
Set Construction	**Splinter**
Sound Operator	**Marc Williams**
Lighting Operator	**Andy Webster**
Dramaturg	**Suzanne Bell**

Cast

Brid Brennan
Millie Sildness

Brid's theatre credits include:
Doubt (Abbey Theatre Dublin);
Pillars of the Community and
Rutherford & Son (National
Theatre); *Little Foxes, A Kind of
Alaska* and *The Dark* (Donmar
Warehouse); *La Lupa* and *Macbeth*
(RSC); *Smelling a Rat* (Hampstead
Theatre); *Dancing at Lughansa*
(International tour – 1992 Tony
Award Best Featured Actress);
Woman & Scarecrow and
Bailegangaire (Royal Court); *By the
Bog of Cats* and *Absolutely (Perhaps)!*
(Wyndham's); *Edward II*
(Manchester Royal Exchange) and
Playboy of the Western World (Druid
Theatre).

Television credits include*: Sunday,
Any Time Now,Cracker, Tell Tale
Hearts, Four Days in July,
Ghostwatch* and *Ballroom of
Romance.*

Film credits include: *Felicia's
Journey, Topsy Turvy, Dancing at
Lughnasa* (1999 IFTA Best Actress
Award Winner), *Trojan Eddie,
Guinevere* and *Anne Devlin.*

Brendan Conroy
Fergal Monahan

Brendan's theatre credits include:
*Playboy of the Western World,
Translations, The Field, Mandragola,
Calvary, The Hostage* and *Cuirt an
Mhean Oiche* (Abbey Theatre,
Dublin); *Kings of the Kilburn High
Road, Talbot's Box, Moonshine* and
Bent (Red Kettle); *Dracula, Famine*
and *The Beggars Opera* (Druid
Theatre Company); *The Tempest*
(Corcadorca); *Silas Mariner* and
Oedipus Rex (Storytellers); *Juno and
the Paycock* (Northern Stage); *Who's
Afraid of Virgina Woolf?* (Plush) and
Belfry (LivinDred).

Television credits include:
*Rock Rivals, Prosperity, Ballykissangel,
Sailortown, The Lilac Bus, The Irish
R.M.* and *Ros na Rún.*

Film credits include: *Kings, A Love
Divided, The General, Butcher Boy,
Moll Flanders, Circle of Friends,
Secret of Roan Inish, A Man of No
Importance* and *The Bounty.*

Cast

Matthew Dunphy
Ruairi McLoughlin

Matthew's theatre credits include:
Port Authority (Liverpool Everyman); *The Boy Soldier* (Red Kettle); *Under The Black Flag* and *Coriolanus* (Globe Theatre); *You Never Can Tell* (Garrick Theatre and Bath Theatre Royal); *The Quare Fellow* (Oxford Stage Company); *Purgatory* and *The Dandy Dolls* (Abbey Theatre, Dublin); *The Lieutenant of Inishmore* (Tour); *The Day I Swapped My Dad For Two Goldfish* (The Ark); *Sons and Daughters* (The Peacock) and *A Christmas Carol* (The Gate).

Television credits include: *Macbeth* and *Fair City*.

Kristofer Gummerus
Brynjar Sildness

Kristofer studied at Guildhall School of Music and Drama where his credits include *Measure for Measure, Afore Night Come, Half a Sixpence, The Memory of Water, Richard III* and *Oedipus Rex*.

Kristofer's theatre credits include:
Cyrano de Bergerac and *Not The End of The World* (Bristol Old Vic); *Daughters of the North* (The Fins Theatre Company); *Peer Gynt* (Dale Teater Kompani); *No Pasaran* and *The Sea* (Finn-Brit Players) and *The Prince and the Pauper* (Pavana Produccions).

Film credits include: *Pieta, Midnight Mosaic* and *Trace*.

Emily Taaffe
Niamh McLoughlin

Emily studied at The London
Academy of Music and Dramatic Art
where her credits include *The Cherry
Orchard, Henry IV, After October,
Otto Klump, Breakfast at Tiffanys*
and *War*.

She also studied at Trinity College
Dublin where her credits include
Medea, 4.48 Psychosis, Far Away
and *Self-Accusation*.

This is Emily's first professional
production.

Company

Lizzie Nunnery
Writer

Lizzie was one of the four writers on
the Amnesty Freedom of Expression
Award-winning *Unprotected*,
performed in 2006 at the Everyman
and the Edinburgh Fringe Festival.

A graduate of the Everyman and
Playhouse Young Writers Group,
Lizzie is a former Henry Cotton
Writer on Attachment at the
Theatres. She was also one of seven
writers on attachment to Paines
Plough Theatre Company under the
2006 Future Perfect scheme and was
one of the BBC/London Royal
Court 50 to support emerging
talent across the country. Her first
play, *The Fine Art of Falling to Pieces*,
was one of the winners of
the Oxford Student New Writing
Competition, 2003 and was
produced in Oxford and at the
Edinburgh Festival.

Other previous works include *Love*
and *Dragon Fruit*, both of which
have received rehearsed readings at
the Everyman theatre. Her short
play *Wicked Women* was performed
as part of The Miniaturists event at
the 2007 Everyword festival of new
writing.

She is currently under commission to
BBC Radio 4.

Company

Gemma Bodinetz
Director

Gemma Bodinetz took up her post as Artistic Director for the Liverpool Everyman and Playhouse in September 2003. Since then she has directed *The Kindness of Strangers* and *The Mayor of Zalamea* at the Everyman; *Ma Rainey's Black Bottom, Who's Afraid of Virginia Woolf?, The Lady of Leisure* and *All My Sons* at the Playhouse, and *Yellowman* on tour.

Gemma has previously worked at The Royal Court Theatre, London, leaving briefly to assist Harold Pinter on *The Caretaker* before returning to co-direct *Hush* with Max Stafford-Clark. She then moved on to become freelance director and Associate Director at Hampstead Theatre.

Gemma's directing credits include: *Caravan* and *A Buyers Market* (The Bush Theatre); *Yard Gal* (Royal Court , London and MCC New York); *Breath Boom* (The Royal Court, London); *Hamlet* (Bristol Old Vic); *Luminosity* (Royal Shakespeare Company); *Rosencrantz and Guildenstern are Dead* and *Four Knights in Knaresborough* (West Yorkshire Playhouse); *Paper Husband, Chimps, English Journeys, Snake* and *After the Gods* (Hampstead Theatre); *Shopping and Fucking* (New York Theatre Workshop); *Closer to Heaven* (West End) and *Guiding Star* (Liverpool Everyman and National Theatre).

Ruari Murchison
Designer

Ruari has designed productions at The Stratford Festival (Canada), Washington DC, Stuttgart, Luzern and Haarlem. UK work includes productions at The National Theatre, Royal Court, The Young Vic, The Royal Shakespeare Company, Nottingham Playhouse, West Yorkshire Playhouse, Bristol Old Vic and on many tours.

Recent design credits include: *Mappa Mundi, Frozen, The Waiting Room* and *The Red Balloon* (National Theatre); *Titus Andronicus* (Royal Shakespeare Company); *The Solid Gold Cadillac* (Garrick); *A Busy Day* (Lyric, Shaftesbury Avenue); *Peggy Sue Got Married* (Shaftesbury Theatre); *The Snowman* (Peacock); *West Side Story* and *The Sound of Music* (Stratford Festival, Canada); *Henry IV parts 1 and 2* (Washington DC); *Hamlet* (Birmingham Rep, National Tour and Elisnore, Denmark); *Der Freischutz* (Finnish National Opera); *Peter Grimes* and *Cosi fan Tutte* (Luzerner Opera); *La Cenerentola* and *Il Barbiere di Siviglia* (Garsington); *The Protecting Veil* (Birmingham Royal Ballet) and *Landschaft und Erinnerung* (Stuttgart Ballett).

Ruari's designs for *Racing Demon, The Absence of War* and *Murmuring Judges* at Birmingham Rep were nominated for the TMA Best Design award in 2003.

Conor Linehan
Composer

Conor Linehan has composed scores for theatres throughout Ireland and Britain.

Theatre Credits Include: *The Lady of Leisure* (Liverpool Playhouse); *Macbeth, Two Gentlemen of Verona, Edward the Third, Loveplay* and *Luminosity* (Royal Shakespeare Company); *Peer Gynt* and *Playboy of the Western World* (National Theatre); *The Wake, Saint Joan, The Colleen Bawn, Love in the Title, The Tempest, She Stoops to Conquer, The Cherry Orchard, Homeland* and *The School for Scandal* (Abbey Theatre, Dublin); *A View From The Bridge* and *Long Days Journey Into Night* (Gate Theatre, Dublin); *Everyday* and *Dublin By Lamplight* (Corn Exchange); *Antigone* and *The Crock of Gold* (Storytellers); *Mermaids* (Coisceim Dance Theatre); *Rebecca* (David Pugh Ltd); *Rosencrantz and Guildenstern are Dead* and *Four Knights At Knaresborough* (West Yorkshire Playhouse); *The Mayor of Zalamea* (Liverpool Everyman); *Carthiginians* and *A Dolls House* (The Lyric Theatre Belfast) and *Twelfth Night* (Thelma Holt productions).

Conor also works as a concert pianist in which capacity he performs an extensive solo and chamber music repertoire.

Fergus O'Hare
Sound Designer

Fergus has worked on numerous productions for the National Theatre, Royal Shakespeare Company, Donmar Warehouse and the Old Vic.

Most recent work includes: *The Entertainer* (Old Vic); *The Electric Hills* (Liverpool Everyman); *Our Country's Good* (Liverpool Playhouse); *King Lear* and *The Seagull* (Royal Shakespeare Company and World Tour); *The New Statesman* (Trafalgar Studios); *Rabbit* (59E59 Theatre New York); *Whipping It Up* (Bush Theatre and New Ambassadors); *Improbable Frequency* (Traverse Theatre); *Fool For Love* and *Who's Afraid of Virgina Woolf?* (Apollo Theatre) and *See How They Run* (Duchess Theatre.

Work in New York, Los Angeles and Sydney includes: *Hecuba, The Shape of Things, A Day in the Death of Joe Egg, Dance of Death, Noises Off, An Enemy of the People* and *Electra,* for which Fergus received a Drama Desk nomination.

Company

Paul Keogan
Lighting Designer

Paul's recent theatre credits include:
Woyzeck (Corcadora Theatre Company); *Julius Caesar, School for Scandal, Homeland, The Dandy Dolls, Portia Coughlan, Beauty in a Broken Place, Cúirt an Mheán Oíche, Heavenly Bodies* and *The Cherry Orchard* (Abbey Theatre, Dublin); *Festen, Performances* and *Gates of Gold* (The Gate, Dublin); *Smaller* (Lyric Theatre and tour); *Harvest* (Royal Court); *Blue/Orange* (Sheffield Crucible); *Woyzeck* (Corcadora Theatre Company); *The Tempest* (UK Tour); *Born Bad* and *In Arabia* (Hampstead Theatre); *Shimmer* and *Olga* (Traverse, Edinburgh); *Too Late for Logic* (Kings Theatre, Edinburgh); *The Silver Tassie* (Almeida Theatre); *The Walworth Farce* and *The Spirit of Annie Ross* (Druid).

Recent opera credits include:
The Lighthouse (Montepulciano, Italy); *Der Silbersee, Rusalka, Don Gregorio, Transformations, Penelope* and *Susannah* (Wexford Opera Festival); *The Makropulos Case, Un Ballo in Maschera* and *Der Fliegende Holländer* (Opera Zuid, Netherlands) *The Queen of Spades, L'Elisir d'Amore, Lady Macbeth of Mtensk* and *The Silver Tassie* (Opera Ireland) and *Pierrot Lunaire* (Almeida Opera).

Paul is an associate artist of the Abbey Theatre Dublin.

Jacquie Davies
Costume Supervisor

Jacquie's theatre credits include:
The Way Home, The Morris and *Port Authority* (Liverpool Everyman); *Our Country's Good* (Liverpool Playhouse); *Vurt, Wise Guys, Unsuitable Girls* and *Perfect* (Contact Theatre, Manchester); *Oleanna* (Clwyd Theatr Cymru); *Love on the Dole* (Lowry); *Never the Sinner* (Library Theatre) and *Shockheaded Peter* (West End).

Opera includes work at: Scottish Opera, Buxton Opera Festival, Music Theatre Wales and Opera Holland Park.

Television and film includes:
Queer as Folk, The Parole Officer, I Love The 1970's, I Love The 1980's, Brookside and *Hollyoaks*.

Lucy Kerbel
Assistant Director

Lucy's directing credits include:
Mouse (Underbelly, Edinburgh);
Is Everyone OK? (Latitude Festival);
Extracts from *East is East* (Royal
Court Open House); *Much Ado
About Nothing* and *Romeo and Juliet*
(Ripley Castle); *Guy Fawkes Night*
(Old Vic 24Hour Plays); *Play*
(Trafalgar Studios); *Jimmy Cliff*
and *Red* (Theatre 503); *Multiplex*
(Lyric Hammersmith); *My London*
(Diorama) and *Love and Money*
(Young Vic).

**Credits as Assistant Director
include:** *Attempts on Her Life* and
Waves (National Theatre); *Hamlet*
(New Ambassadors); *Bone* (Royal
Court Upstairs) and *Hamlet*
(English Touring Theatre).

**Workshop and rehearsed reading
credits include:** *Going After Alice*
(Old Vic at Theatre Row, New
York); *Camembert, The Chieftains
Daughteri, Salonika* and *The Hour
We Knew Nothing of Each Other*
(National Theatre Studio) and
Through The Night (Royal Court).

Ginny Schiller
Casting Director

Ginny's theatre credits include:
The May Queen (Liverpool
Everyman); *All My Sons* (Liverpool
Playhouse); *Imagine This* (Theatre
Royal, Plymouth); *The Giant*
(Hampstead); *The Changeling,
French without Tears, Someone Else's
Shoes, Mother Courage, The Old
Country, Hamlet, Rosencrantz and
Guildenstern are Dead* and *Twelfth
Night* (as Casting Associate for
English Touring Theatre); *Stockholm*
(Frantic Assembly); *Dancing at
Lughnasa* (Lyric Theatre, Belfast);
The Last South (Pleasance,
Edinburgh Festival); *The Canterbury
Tales* and *Complete Works Festival*
(Royal Shakespeare Company);
Macbeth and *How Many Miles to
Basra?* (West Yorkshire Playhouse);
The Taming of the Shrew (Wilton's
Music Hall); *Dr Faustus* and *The
Taming of the Shrew* (Bristol Old
Vic); *A Passage to India* (Shared
Experience); *Macbeth* (Albery) and
extensive work at Soho, Chichester
and the Royal Shakespeare
Company.

Television and film credits include:
*The Kingdom, Notes on a Scandal,
George Orwell - A Life in Pictures*
(Emmy Award Winner), *The Bill*
and *The Falklands Play*.

Radio credits include: *Felix Holt the
Radical, The Pickwick Papers, Tender
is the Night* and *The Bride's
Chamber*.

Staff

Leah Abbott Box Office Assistant, **Vicky Adlard** Administrator, **Laura Arends** Marketing Campaigns Manager, **Deborah Aydon** Executive Director, **Lindsey Bell** Technician, **Suzanne Bell** Literary Manager, **Serdar Bilis** Associate Director, **Gemma Bodinetz** Artistic Director, **Julie Burrow** Theatre and Community Assistant, **Moira Callaghan** Theatre and Community Administrator, **Colin Carey** Security Officer, **Joe Cornmell** Finance Assistant, **Stephen Dickson** Finance Assistant, **Angela Dooley** Cleaning Staff, **Alison Eley** Finance Assistant, **Roy Francis** Maintenance Technician, **Rosalind Gordon** Deputy Box Office Manager, **Mike Gray** Deputy Technical Stage Manager, **Helen Grey** Stage Door Receptionist, **Helen Griffiths** House Manager, **Jayne Gross** Development Manager, **Poppy Harrison** Box Office Assistant, **Stuart Holden** IT and Communications Manager, **David Jordan** Fire Officer, **Sarah Kelly** Assistant House Manager, **Sue Kelly** Cleaning Staff, **Steven Kennett** Assistant Maintenance Technician (Performance), **Sven Key** Fire Officer, **Lynn-Marie Kilgallon** Internal Courier/Receptionist, **Andrew King** Stage Door Receptionist, **Gavin Lamb** Marketing Communications Officer, **Rachel Littlewood** Community Outreach Co-ordinator, **Robert Longthorne** Building Development Director, **Howard Macaulay** Deputy Chief Technician (Stage), **Ged Manson** Cleaning Staff, **Christine Mathews-Sheen** Director of Finance and Administration, **Jason McQuaide** Technical Stage Manager (Playhouse), **Dan Meigh** Youth Theatre Director, **Liz Nolan** Assistant to the Directors, **Lizzie Nunnery** Literary Assistant, **Patricia O'Brien** Cleaning Staff, **Vivien O'Callaghan** Youth Theatre Administrator, **Sarah Ogle** Marketing Director, **Sean Pritchard** Senior Production Manager, **Collette Rawlinson** Stage Door Receptionist, **Victoria Rope** Programme Co-ordinator, **Rebecca Ross-Williams** Theatre and Community Director, **Jeff Salmon** Technical Director, **Hayley Sephton** House Manager, **Steve Sheridan** Assistant Maintenance Technician, **Jackie Skinner** Education Co-ordinator, **Louise Sutton** Box Office Supervisor, **Jennifer Tallon-Cahill** Deputy Chief Electrician, **Matthew Taylor** Marketing and Press Assistant, **Pippa Taylor** Press and Media Officer, **Marie Thompson** Cleaning Supervisor/Receptionist, **Scott Turner** Market Planning Manager, **Paul Turton** Finance Manager, **Andy Webster** Lighting Technician, **Marc Williams** Chief Technician (Everyman), **Emma Wright** Production Manager.

Thanks to all our Front of House team and casual Box Office staff.

Board Members:
Cllr Warren Bradley, Professor Michael Brown (Chair), Mike Carran, Michelle Charters, Rod Holmes, Vince Killen, Professor E. Rex Makin, Andrew Moss, Roger Phillips, Sara Williams, Ivan Wadeson.

The regulations of Liverpool City Council provide that:
The public may leave at the end of the performance by all exit doors and all exit doors must at that time be open. Note: all Liverpool theatres can be emptied in three minutes or less if the audience leaves in an orderly manner. All gangways, passages, staircases and exits must be kept entirely free from obstruction. Persons shall not be permitted to stand or sit in any of the intersecting gangways or stand in any unseated space in the auditorium unless standing in such space has been authorised by the City Council.

SMOKING AND DRINKING GLASSES ARE NOT ALLOWED IN THE AUDITORIUM AT ANY TIME.

We would like to remind you that the bleep of digital watches, pagers and mobile phones during the performance may distract the actors and your fellow audience members. Please ensure they are switched off for the duration of the performance. You are strongly advised not to leave bags and other personal belongings unattended anywhere in the theatre.

Lizzie Nunnery
Intemperance

ff

faber and faber

First published in 2007
by Faber and Faber Limited
3 Queen Square, London WC1N 3AU

Typeset by Country Setting, Kingsdown, Kent CT14 8ES
Printed in the UK by CPI Bookmarque, Croydon, CR0 4TD

A CIP record for this book
is available from the British Library

ISBN 978–0–571–23814–9

2 4 6 8 10 9 7 5 3 1

For my Dad,
and for his Dad who played the piano

Acknowledgements

Suzanne Bell for dramaturgy, research,
encouragement and support

Gemma Bodinetz for supporting
the idea from the beginning

Professor John Belchem and Dr Sally Sheard
for their invaluable research assistance

Vidar Norheim for research assistance,
Norwegian translations and endless patience

Rita Nunnery for always being interested

Characters

Millie Sildnes
thirty-five

Brynjar Sildnes
her husband, twenty-five

Fergal Monahan
Millie's father, fifty-five

Niamh McLoughlin
Millie's daughter by her first husband, sixteen

Ruairi McLoughlin
Millie's son by her first husband, fifteen

Setting

Liverpool, September 1854,
Hockenhall Court, off Dale Street.
A cellar room leading into a slum court.

INTEMPERANCE

The opinion of the many middle-class observers was
that the lot of the poor was not the consequence
of poverty, but of that which creates poverty;
that is improvidence, indolence and, most of all,
intemperance.

Anthony Miller, *Poverty Deserved:*
Relieving the Poor in Victorian Liverpool

Act One

SCENE ONE: IMPRUDENCE

Early evening. It's raining. An incredibly old and disintegrating piano sits against one wall, so rotten it looks ready to collapse. Millie, five months pregnant and slightly showing, is sitting at the table, carefully separating an old and battered rope and collecting the extracted oakum material. Ruairi is lying against the wall. A tin bucket collects drops from a leak in the ceiling, in a tight rhythm. Fergal lies, skeleton-like, on an old mattress, wheezing deeply. His eyes remain half shut throughout the scene. A fiddle is being played in the next room accompanied by raucous intermittent singing. Here and throughout the play we hear the almost imperceptible buzz of flies.

Fergal Fella was in here today, um –

Millie Doctor?

Fergal Nuisance fella.

Millie Who?

Fergal Calls himself the Inspector of Nuisances or some such.

Millie Oh, I know the cheeky old crow. Jesus, we're a nuisance now?

Fergal Says we have te limewash the place.

Millie Did he say why?

Fergal Three more went yesterday. Alison Donnell's dead of it.

Millie Jesus.

Ruairi It's not round here yet.

Fergal Says we have te limewash the place.

Millie She'd a been what; thirteen?

Ruairi Ye know who's bringing it.

Fergal I told him we're only buying what we can eat or drink at present and I don't much fancy a limewash sandwich.

Millie You never.

Fergal No.

Ruairi They should be bleedin kickin them back in the water.

Millie (*to Ruairi*) Don't start.

Ruairi Everyone's sayin: they're bringing it over on the boats.

Millie You wanna set the world te rights; start by earnin, so yer family can eat.

Ruairi Can't work if there's no work in.

Millie There was the rest of the cotton load, ye said so.

Ruairi I wasn't picked.

Millie Course ye weren't picked, ye were standing on the docks swayin and sweatin with a hangover, stinkin of last night's ale.

Ruairi It's not something I'm doin; hundreds were turned away.

Millie Hundreds weren't crawlin round the floor in here last night like a bloody dog.

Ruairi Jay Finny says they want us drunk.

Millie They what?

Ruairi They *want* me drunk.

Millie Who? God and all his angels?

Ruairi Council, Finny says.

Millie Well I must say, they're doing a great job.

Ruairi They don't do a great job at nothing.

Millie Here we go.

Ruairi All that money they've got, and a *hall*'s what they make?

Millie I'll buy yer a soapbox fer Christmas, hey?

Ruairi I said that to Finny – what's a *hall* to us?

Millie Aye, what *is* it to you?

Ruairi They can build a thing like that, all pillars and faces of fellas with beards and – like some bastard's castle – and they can't make that tap run clean? (*Pointing outside into the court.*)

Millie Ruairi, if that tap out there ran with God's own holy water you'd still be lying on yer back singin hymns through a whiskey bottle.

Ruairi I never sang a hymn in my life.

Fergal Mrs Donnell was in here, with a bucket, collecting fer the funeral.

Millie Jesus.

Fergal She can't afford te bury the child.

Millie And the nuisance inspector fella, he told yer it was the cholera?

Fergal Aye.

Millie It's like last time. I told ye, didn't I? I could smell it on the air.

Fergal He goes, 'If you place any value on your lives, you'll limewash the place.' I said, 'If you place any value on *your* life ye'll piss off out of the place.'

Millie Ye didn't?

Fergal No.

Ruairi Ye know who's bringin it.

Millie Don't start, Ruairi.

Ruairi The bleedin Poles and the Krauts and the rest of the swill of them; fallin off the boats stinkin of it.

Fergal What's he sayin?

Millie He's not sayin anything, Da.

Ruairi Jay Finny says –

Millie Jay Finny spends so much money in The Pig and Whistle, they treat him to room service whilst he takes a piss.

Ruairi He's something to say about the bleedin Scandies.

Fergal Mill, stop bending your back over that.

Millie (*to Ruairi*) You spent less time in The Grapes, and more out earnin –

Ruairi Can't work if they won't give me work.

Millie You're like a beggar bangin out yer one grating tune –

Ruairi Two whole sugar-loads went to the water last night – bleedin storms –

Fergal (*making the sign of the cross superstitiously*) God protect their souls.

Ruairi The wind blows the wrong way on the water and I go hungry to bed: how's that?

Millie Tell ye what, why don't ye round up the council and the drink and the wind and give 'em each a good smack in the eye, 'stead of bringing your black heart home to us?

Fergal Dora through there says Annie McLennan's been in nick.

Millie (*alert to this*) How's that?

Fergal Old Annie's had a lifetime of black luck –

Millie Just tell me what happened.

Fergal The Ministry to the Poor's been up Fontenoy Street giving handouts: thee come to Annie's an she's down on her old broken knees begging fer a bit of coal and a morsel of bread –

Millie The woman lives on the side of a midden; ye wouldna thought it'd leave her with an appetite –

Fergal The kids all round her feet gnashing their teeth and grabbin their stomachs –

Millie Don't exaggerate, Da – Dora never said that.

Fergal They were hungry anyhow and had their little hands outstretched for mercy –

Millie (*irritated*) Da –

Fergal Anyhow, those charity fellas had no sooner set foot in the room than they smelt the whiff of rum off old Annie, and turned right back round again –

Ruairi Bastards –

Millie I'll bet she lost it –

Fergal Old Annie may only have one tooth, but Dora swears that tooth was embedded in that Reverend's neck – and she heard it from Cora Hanlon who saw the whole thing.

Millie Cora Hanlon doesn't live on Fontenoy Street.

Fergal Well, she heard it from Bridie O'Brien.

Ruairi Bunch of bastards –

Millie They won't help them as they see won't help themselves; simple as that.

Ruairi The money they've got they should be buying us all a round.

Fergal Leave off that, Mill, ye've had no rest all day –

Millie (*to Fergal*) Are you gonna do this for me?

Fergal Ye've a baby there te think of –

Millie (*sarcastic*) Really, Da? I'd totally forgotten.

Fergal Let Brynjar do it.

Millie Brynjar's been out all day earnin for us –

Ruairi I wasn't *picked*.

Brynjar enters, bouncing off the soles of his feet with delight, with a crate of bananas in one hand and his other hand behind his back. He immediately plants a kiss on Millie's cheek and, as he does so, hands a bottle of whiskey from behind his back to Fergal, who hides it in his covers. Ruairi watches unamused.

Millie Fell off a boat? (*Kissing him on the cheek in return.*)

Brynjar Ten thousand of them. All overripe. They're wild trying to clear them by morning. Ye should see it, men swimming in bananas, breaking their backs like slaves.

Millie What's banana in Norwegian?

Brynjar No man has ever set eyes on a banana in Norway.

Ruairi snorts critically through a mouthful of banana.

(*To Millie.*) The whole lot nearly went splat.

Millie Went what now?

Brynjar Bricks – (*Gesturing, indicating its close proximity.*) On Dale Street I walked under the ladders, where they're building the Globe – the insurance place – I duck under in a hurry – and looking up I see bricks – a great weight of bricks falling towards me, on every side –

Millie (*going to him and wiping down dust from his coat*) Jesus, Brynjar, you're no good to me dead.

Brynjar I can't move any way, or another brick hits me, so I stand. And they scream at me but the bricks fall everywhere that I'm not, and me and the bananas – (*Beat.*) are whole.

Millie (*hugs him quickly and roughly*) One day your charm'll wear off.

Brynjar (*rubbing Millie's tummy*) How is my little one growing?

Millie (*sarcastic*) Haven't had a chance to ask.

Brynjar (*to Millie*) You go for a walk with me later?

Millie Have the docks people said anything about next week? Are they keeping you on?

Brynjar You don't worry about that. You go for a walk with me.

Millie I know what kinda walk you mean.

Ruairi makes a disgusted noise, returning to his position against the wall. He begins to bang his foot against the tin bucket, forming a syncopated rhythm with the noise of the water. Brynjar laughs and fetches writing paper and a pen from a pile in the corner.

Millie More lies for Papa?

Brynjar I give comfort to an old man.

Ruairi . . . this shite.

Brynjar begins to write, still standing, performing for the room.

Brynjar 'Dearest Father' –

Millie Dearest Pappy.

Brynjar 'Dearest Papa, Virginia is a vast land of hope.'

Fergal Virginia now?

Brynjar A passenger ship goes tomorrow. Harry promised to post it for me.

Fergal What do you know about Virginia?

Brynjar What does my papa know about Virginia? (*Writing*) 'Virginia is a vast land of hope.'

Millie Don't write it twice.

Ruairi I spoke to the guy, Ma, there's no work coming in.

Fergal I can tell you about Virginia from the mouth of a man who's walked in the dust of it.

Brynjar (*his hands over his ears*) No, Fergal! No! Don't spoil my picture please.

Fergal Nothing going for the authority of age I suppose.

Brynjar (*composes in his head a few moments, humming energetically*) 'It is all I hoped for and all I dreamed beside. The rooms are . . .'

Ruairi Ma, de ye hear me?

Millie 'Softer beds than –' (*Searches for the metaphor.*) What's soft?

Ruairi With the weather as it is, he said it could be weeks.

Brynjar 'I have no rooms. The sky is my leaking roof.'

Ruairi There mightn't be a ship for weeks.

Fergal Ha hah. 'The sky is my leaking roof.' I like that. Ye read that?

Ruairi Ma?

Millie (*to Ruairi*) Hey?

Brynjar 'The sea is like silk skirts on a pale thigh.'

Millie (*distracted, laughing*) Filthy bastard.

Fergal No sea in Virginia.

   Ruairi bangs louder on the tin.

Brynjar (*writing*) 'The sea is bluer than I've ever seen.'

Ruairi Ye think the ol bastard won't see through ye?

Brynjar He's a believer. (*Beat.*) 'The sand is like walking on . . .'

Ruairi Crushed glass.

Brynjar Too painful.

Ruairi (*sarcastic*) Ye think?

Brynjar (*writes while he talks*) He waits hungry for news of my life in America: I feed his mind with hope. (*He reads aloud as he writes.*) 'Today I received a letter from New York telling me that they have built me a monument.'

Beat. They all look at him in disbelief. He writes frantically.

'They have built me a statue in my image, to mark my great service to society.'

Millie De ye not think yer pushing yer pappy's faith a bit far?

Brynjar Last letter I talked the whole long tale of how in New York I went to shake hands with the mayor for persuading a thousand of the New Yorkers away from the evils of drink –

Millie They wouldn't give yer a statue so quick –

Brynjar I tell him that they call me the king of the temperance movement.

Fergal (*sarcastic*) I'll drink te that.

Brynjar I am a hero to him if I write this.

Millie Jesus, is there nothing more exciting he'd like te hear? Can ye not tell him ye fought in a battle or some such?

Brynjar 'Papa, when I spoke to the crowds they fell down crying with shame and came fighting each other to sign the pledge to drink no more.'

Fergal I don't reckon thee'd give yer a statue.

Brynjar Fifty feet. With two crouching angels either side.

Millie Why not make the whole thing a lot easier and tell him ye in fact never got near America, as ye found yerself a wonderful wife here in Liverpool?

Fergal (*pondering the issue*) No, ye need te've been in some form of war te get a statue.

*The fiddle stops playing. Through the thin wall we
hear it twang as it hits the floor. Screams, muffled
shouts.*

Ruairi (*pulling himself up*) Bleedin idiots. I'm meeting
Finny.

*Ruairi sets about pulling his hat and coat on. He stops
as Fergal begins to splutter forcefully.*

Brynjar You want water?

Fergal shakes his head.

Ruairi From the tap in the court? Ye wanna kill him
straight off?

*Fergal begins to cough and heave for breath with
frightening violence. Millie jumps up to attend to him.*

Millie God, Da, less of this–

*She whacks him heavily on the back. He continues to
cough.*

Fer God's sake, Da . . .

*Fergal shrugs her off and, in one motion, pulls out the
whiskey, unscrews it and drinks from it, lying back
gasping for air. A moment of stunned silence. Turning
on Ruairi.*

Where the bleedin hell'd he get that from?

Brynjar He's breathing now.

Millie We've no money. We've no money for this.
(*Grabbing him by the clothes.*)

Ruairi I didn't –

Millie Did ye steal it?

Ruairi No!

Millie Did ye?

Ruairi It was him! Your Viking boy there –

Brynjar Millie, he didn't –

Fergal lies still, gasping. He tries to signal it was Brynjar who gave it to him, but it goes unnoticed.

Millie Ye must think I'm stupid.

Ruairi If I had a bottle of whiskey I'd not be hiding it in an old man's bed.

Brynjar Millie, it wasn't –

Millie Is that the kind of name you want to get this family when Brynjar's out there working to –?

Ruairi *I'm* out there working!

Brynjar (*attempting to cut through*) They gave me a new job.

Millies turns, confused.

I didn't want you to be disappointed so –

Millie Ye what?

Brynjar They gave me a new job.

Millie Gave ye . . . Who gave ye . . .?

Brynjar The Globe Insurance Company.

Beat. Ruairi reacts physically.

I thought, I'll wait. The worst thing would be if –

Millie A job?

Brynjar A clerk.

Millie You're already a clerk.

Brynjar A permanent job as a clerk.

Millie Oh my God . . .

Brynjar Eighty-five pounds a year.

Millie Oh my God.

Brynjar I start in three days' time.

She stands in shock.

I hid it to surprise you. (*Beat.*) The whiskey.

Millie (*roused suddenly, shaking Fergal*) Da. Da, de ye hear it? De ye hear this? (*To Brynjar.*) How much?

Brynjar Eighty-five pounds a year.

Millie (*to Fergal*) Ye hear that, Da?

Fergal coughs and nods enthusiastic recognition, not yet up to speech and all the while watching Ruairi.

Brynjar You remember Mr Thompson who spoke to us once in the street?

Millie The man with the beautiful shoes.

Brynjar Mr Thompson, he has his hand on my back. He said, 'Welcome to the City of Gentlemen.'

Millie shrieks in delight. Brynjar does an exaggerated impression of a sombre, well-spoken voice:

'In Manchester they are involved in the dirty process of making things, here we are involved in the glorious process of moving things.'

Millie What'll ye be moving?

Brynjar Ships! We will all be moving ships.

Millie How'll ye be doing that?

Brynjar I'll be doing accounts.

Millie This is really true?

He nods.

No one's had a real job in this family for twenty years. Twenty years wouldn't ye say, Da? (*Going to Brynjar and pulling at his slightly worn suit.*) Your suit: ye'll need a new suit. Ye can't start a job like that. We can pawn something.

Brynjar (*taking off his heavy coat and throwing it down triumphantly*) I'll pawn my coat!

Millie Your father's coat?

Brynjar I'll buy *three* coats before winter!

Millie And ye'll need new shoes if you're gonna be standing next to men like that. You'll need – (*Beat. Struck suddenly.*) We can move.

Brynjar Of course we'll move.

Millie Where'll we move?

Brynjar (*laughing*) I don't know yet –

Millie But not in the courts?

Brynjar Of course not in the courts. Somewhere high up with a window –

Millie gasps in delight.

And we'll open the window and let in the air, and we'll wave to people in the street, and there'll be light and lots of rooms – three rooms perhaps –

Millie No.

Brynjar Yes.

Millie High up?

Brynjar Why not!

Millie Ruairi, ye hear?

Ruairi I can hear.

Millie Ye hear we're moving? We're *moving*.

Ruairi (*staring intensely at Brynjar*) Ye shouldn't believe 'em. They talk shit. All the time, promising things, especially to foreigners. They love to do over the foreigners.

Brynjar They swore to me it was –

Ruairi (*pulling away from Millie*) Well, of course they bastard swore. Of course they did. Why would they not . . . Why would they . . . ?

Millie turns to Brynjar, laughing ecstatically. Brynjar lifts her up and shakes her, making her laugh more. Ruairi kicks the bucket against the wall in a sudden fit of rage, water flying in all directions, and stalks to the door.

Millie (*calling to Ruairi*) How aren't ye happy?

Ruairi I am happy. I'm bloody ecstatic.

He exits angrily. Millie stands dazed. Brynjar goes to her and hugs her tightly.

Millie This is true?

He nods again, laughing.

You're a miracle. You're not a man, you're a miracle. (*Beat.*) This is true?

Brynjar (*kissing her*) I promise. (*Beat.*) I promise.

Millie Ye promise me?

Brynjar I promise.

They hug. Fergal continues to gasp. A baby cries unattended in the next room. Lights down. We hear the sound effect of a tidal wave approaching, growing to a deafening level before subsiding slowly.

SCENE TWO: IMPROPREITY

It is one o'clock the following morning. Fergal lies sleeping in his bed, wheezing loudly and whistling through his nose. Millie and Brynjar lie behind the dividing curtain, their bed being an overturned cellar door roughly covered. Millie sleeps while Brynjar sits upright, unable to sleep for Fergal's breathing.

Brynjar (*whispering*) Shut up. Please shut up. (*Beat.*) Just shut up.

> *Fergal stops breathing suddenly. Brynjar listens, at first with a relieved sense of disbelief and then with a gradual panic. He starts up from the bed just as Fergal suddenly gasps and begins his whistling and snorting again. Sitting down he leans his face against Millie's belly, listening to the heartbeat. He begins to sing a traditional Norwegian song, 'En villand svømmer stille', to her stomach, quietly at first then louder as he forgets himself.*

Og fuglen kan ei drage
Til redens lune skjød,
Og fuglen vil ei klage
Sin smerte og sin nød.

> *Finally he sings sitting upright with his eyes closed and Millie, now awake, looks at him bewildered.*

Millie Jesus, it's like sleeping with a feckin sprite or somethin.

Brynjar (*jumps, surprised*) It was for the baby.

Millie Ye should watch I don't have ye carted off for madness.

Brynjar I can't sleep.

Millie I hear it's going around.

Brynjar I close my eyes and I feel as though they're open; as though my new life is already moving before me.

Millie Every time I close my eyes all I see is water.

Brynjar (*closes his eyes*) I see us in a bright, dry room.

Millie Dreamt the leak got worse and the sea burst through the place.

Brynjar Our baby is fat and laughing at me.

Millie Some things ye can't promise.

Brynjar I'm a lucky man.

Millie Alison Donnell now – you watch; it'll have all them Donnells. It's worse than last time already.

Brynjar You don't know that.

Millie How fast can we be gone?

Brynjar A month perhaps; a few weeks. Very soon –

Millie Few weeks was all it *took* te see half this court lying on their backs in the heat, sweating the last bit of life out. It started with one last time: some kid in back Portland Street comes down with a bit of diarrhoea, then she's gone in a matter of days, and everyone's saying it'll be fine, it's miles away from us, it'll never come, and a month later those same people were competing for a grave.

Brynjar (*hugging her tightly*) It's the air. They tell me in work – men who know these things. They say it's the bad smell on the air.

Millie We had a wake across the way – old Mrs Quilligan. All her grandkids got lined up to kiss her goodbye – these tiny things tripping along in line. Following week every one of them was dead. Every one.

Brynjar We get out of here to clean air –

Millie The Poles on the corner are calling it the 'Irish fever'. 'The Irish fever's coming for us.'

Brynjar (*forcefully*) It won't come for *us*.

Millie I'd rather it died inside me than having te watch it shit itself to death.

Brynjar (*moving away from her, angered*) You don't say that. I won't have you think that.

Millie Ye weren't here five years back. Alright? Ye don't know.

Brynjar I know my child will live.

Millie Ye hear all that breathing? Out there in the court, in all the other rooms. When ye stop at night in the silence and allow yerself te listen, an ye hear hundreds of them. Hundreds of people breathing in an out, all of us lying ourselves down the same way with nothing but a few bits of brick to separate us. And then imagine what it is to hear the breathing become moaning, crying, and then imagine that moaning becoming silence.

Brynjar Our baby will never know about these things.

Millie I tried to go to mass last Sunday. A woman at the door turned me out soon as she saw me. She said, 'Ye can't come before God covered in filth.'

Brynjar Millie?

Beat. She looks at him.

Believe me. Believe in this for me; we are starting again.

Millie stares at him a while and smiles. She holds her hand out to him and he accepts it, moving back towards her.

Millie Tell me the story of how we met.

Brynjar We have new stories to tell.

Millie But that was our first.

Brynjar I'll tell you a story about a young man in Sunndalsøra who could not catch his breath when he heard talk of England and American; who would sit at home with his arithmetic when the other boys worked in fields and in fishing boats, because his father told him that one day he would be a gentleman in the New World.

Millie You were standing above me with two black eyes and nothing in yer pockets.

Brynjar He would be drinking with his friends; red in the face with talk of New York and of Liverpool –

Millie Your face was almost caved in ye'd had that bad a beating, and there was I, lying beneath yer on the road, with you grinning all over your broken mouth.

Brynjar (*coaxing, willing her out of her melancholy*) Or we'd whisper like it was a secret. In these places there were the richest men in the world; buildings so beautiful they make a man feel grand just to stand beneath them; shops and banks and bars to get lost in; opera singers performing in great halls; holidays to the beaches where the ladies walk with parasols.

Millie That's not the world ye found.

Brynjar I found a beautiful woman in the gutter. A beautiful drunk laughing at me –

Millie You nearly tripped over me.

Brynjar And I promised myself then that I would find that world for you – I would bring it to you.

Millie Don't talk rubbish; ye never did.

Brynjar Believe me, Millie.

Millie Between you and me da I get nothing but romance and exaggeration –

Brynjar Do you believe me?

Millie (*beat*) I'll try.

He kisses her. She lies down. He resumes his singing as a lullaby.

Og derfor taus den dukker
Dybt i den mørke fjord,
Og bølgen kold sig lukker
Og sletter ut dens spor.

He holds her protectively. She pulls her ragged blanket around her ears. After a moment, Brynjar gets up from the bed and steps about the room distractedly. Seeing his battered suit jacket, he puts it on. He pulls himself up so that he's standing very straight with his chin up. He practises walking up and down in this way. He holds out his hand as if to greet somebody.

Brynjar (*whispered, miming shaking hands*) How do you do? I work for the Globe Insurance Company. (*He tries again, still whispering, this time with a more grave tone of voice.*) How do you do? I'm from the Globe Insurance Company. I'm so very pleased to meet you.

He starts, hearing someone approaching from outside and ducks back behind the curtain. Niamh enters, highly dishevelled and tipsy. She seizes on the whiskey bottle, drinks from it, beginning to take her clothes off, almost as one movement. Brynjar, who has been peering through, looks away embarrassed. Once in her undergarment, she furtively pulls a long red ribbon out of her clothes and ties it in her hair, feeling it to get a sense of how it might look. She hears him shuffling behind the curtain and quickly hides the ribbon again in her clothes. The following conversation takes place in low voices.

Niamh (*to Brynjar*) I hear ye shifting in there.

Brynjar You are okay coming in so late?

Niamh What are you asking me?

Brynjar I'm asking what happened?

Niamh What are you –?

Brynjar For you to be out so late?

Niamh What?

Brynjar Nothing bad happened?

Niamh No. (*Beat.*) Job done, go to sleep.

Brynjar I can't sleep.

Niamh God's sake, stop hidin behind the curtain if you're gonna talk to me.

Brynjar (*emerging*) Sshhh! Your mother sleeps.

Niamh So let her.

Brynjar sits down at the table with her so they can both speak more quietly.

Brynjar Who were you with?

Niamh Who says I was with anyone?

Brynjar You go out alone now?

Niamh Maybe I do.

Brynjar You go out for three hours, *alone*?

Niamh goes to drink again. Brynjar pulls it off her.

It's your mother's.

Niamh Isn't everything?

Brynjar I got it for her because I have a new job. I'm a real clerk now.

Niamh (*sarcastic*) A *real* clerk?

Brynjar I start in three days.

Niamh (*beat*) Yeah?

Brynjar We'll move out of here.

Niamh That'll be nice fer yer new family.

Brynjar For all of us –

Niamh Maybe I've got other plans.

Brynjar Tell me your plans, Niamh.

Beat. She looks him in the eye.

Niamh She's on her best behaviour with you, ye know? Give it six months, ye'll see what she really is.

Brynjar Don't start telling me stories.

Niamh A dirty drunk.

Brynjar I won't hear it tonight.

Niamh She'd be sat up in here every night with me da: they'd be singing and shouting and turning each other black and blue. He loved and hated her all at once, and who could offer an aul drunk any more.

Brynjar She has more now.

Niamh There was a balance to that.

Brynjar I saw you buying liquorice when you should have been at work.

Niamh Me da'd come in here and whip me up off the floor. Walk me through the streets on his shoulders, 'cause we were proud of each other, ye know? Ye ever had that?

Brynjar I've watched you leave in the mornings. You don't go to the refinery.

Niamh We were too low even fer charity – the pair of them always legless and tryna hide it when the Ministry came round. But every time they'd shake their heads and write it down the same: 'Intemperate. This family is incapable of temperance.' Our sin is not that we drink –

Brynjar Niamh –

Niamh But that we can't not drink.

Brynjar How do you have money to buy liquorice?

Niamh Drunks. Dirty drunks.

Brynjar You don't frighten me.

Niamh I do.

Brynjar Niamh –

Niamh I frighten you silent.

Brynjar I have heard men talk about your Mr Adler who runs the sugar refinery.

Niamh Ye've heard what?

Brynjar Everyone hears. The men at work, they talk. He is not a gentleman.

Niamh How awful.

Brynjar This is how you buy your liquorice?

Niamh You wanna watch yerself, Mr Sildnes: yer already startin te think like a rich fella.

Brynjar I don't want to tell Millie.

Niamh Already scared of every whisper and rumour.

Brynjar You are better than this.

Niamh (*enjoying herself*) No, *you're* better than this, *you're* the gentleman, you're the one who's scrambling up that ladder: tryna get respectable. Me? I'm whatever I wanna be.

Brynjar I want to help you.

Niamh Wouldn't it be terrible if it was you those fellas at work were talking about? I don't suppose ye tell them much about the lot of us?

Brynjar (*giving up, angered*) I'm going to sleep.

Niamh You can't sleep.

Brynjar I'm going to.

He goes behind his curtain and lies down, pulling his covers up around his head. Pause.

Niamh Oh, you're proud of us, aren't ye? That's why ye write home a load of lies te Daddy every week, 'cause yer so bloody proud.

Receiving no reply, she sits a few moments watching Fergal. She goes to him and pulls him up in the bed so his breathing eases slightly, still audible but quieter. She takes some money out of her clothing and hides it in a hole in Fergal's mattress. Looking at him for a brief moment more, she whispers:

Night, Fergal.

She grabs the whiskey bottle from the table and exits with it. There is quiet for some moments. We hear the distant sound of a chorus of men, singing a temperance song with drunken enthusiasm:

Throw out the lifeline!
Throw out the lifeline!
Someone is drifting away.

Throw out the lifeline!
Throw out the lifeline!
Someone is sinking today.

The noise fades out and we hear Ruairi shouting goodbyes at a distance. After a few moments he enters quietly, holding a beer bottle in his hand. He goes to the piano and pretends to play, his hands not touching the keys. Brynjar peers out of his curtain again, and returns to bed, once more pulling his covers around his ears. After some time Ruairi begins to knock the bottom of the bottle repeatedly on the table, forcing back emotion. Fergal watches him.

Fergal You pissed, lad?

Ruairi Didn't wanna wake ye.

Fergal Sleepin and wakin's all of a one when ye never rise.

Ruairi Yer a legend in The Grapes ye know, Grand-da? They're all putting bets on when you're gonna go.

Fergal If a man can't provide some gambling speculation in the leaving of his life, what's he really given to the world?

Ruairi Dan Sharkey was near dead in there tonight – ran in to old Owen's pint and watched it shatter against the bar with this look like his whole world was coming loose – he was holding up his hands in apology but Owen was in the mood for it, ye know? The shape of Dan's face when it hit the wall . . . And he was laughin – sat there in his blood, he was laughin. They had to carry him home.

Fergal I'll warrant his mother's not laughing so hard.

Ruairi I envied him.

Fergal There's better ways to know you're alive than chokin on yer tongue on a wet floor.

Ruairi continues to tap the bottle, looking over at the curtain behind which Millie and Brynjar sleep.

Ruairi Spose the pair of them idiots have been bashing glasses to insurance all night?

Fergal Ye'll eat and drink off it, Ruairi, what else are ye worrying for?

Ruairi (*pause as he taps rhythmically*) Ye think he's laughin at me, Grand-da?

Fergal He's sleeping, Ruairi.

Ruairi This old guy – Baines – not old like you, but old, he was up on a chair talking how these fellas who run the docks and the insurance and that – some of them are millionaires, did ye know that?

Fergal I knew that.

Ruairi De ye ever sit and wonder at that kinda thing?

Fergal Did I tell ye about Argentina?

Ruairi You want me te tell ye how much he reckons they spent on that St Whatever's Hall they're opening up – Ye'll fall out ye bed. (*Beat.*) What is it? English guy. Dragon-killer.

Fergal George's.

Ruairi George's Hall. Ye gonna guess at it? Ye wouldn't get it.

Fergal No.

Ruairi He reckons he knows it's more'n a hundred thousand.

Fergal Aye.

Ruairi A *hundred thousand.*

His tapping of the bottle has by now escalated to a violent banging. Fergal puts his hand out and places it on Ruairi's, stopping him.

Fergal God's sake lad, ye'll give yerself a cancer.

Ruairi Ye know there's gonna be *dancin. Dancin.* And brass bands and singers when they open this thing and Tom McKee in the pub – ye know, Niall's lad?

Fergal nods recognition.

He's telling everyone this and he's all excited he might get a look at some of it and I go to him, 'Dancing?' I could be dead in a fortnight if I don't starve first from the filth and the number of these foreign bastards. One of them's in there at me mother each night –

Fergal Where de you think ye come from, tell me that?

Ruairi Why do I wanna see someone dancing?

Fergal Ye've gotta stop actin like a dog with an ulcer over everyone else.

Ruairi (*nodding towards Brynjar*) He'll be out there; cheering and dancing and saying how great everything in this bloody city is.

Fergal Ye can't hate a man fer tryna make something of –

Ruairi I was born here, unlike –

Fergal Unlike *me.* We came from the sea, not the earth. Ye want to think of something big, think of that.

Ruairi It's different with us – This city belongs to the Irish. It can't belong to every other bugger too.

Fergal Can it not?

Ruairi Ye told me about the goat.

Fergal Hah?

Ruairi Argentina. Ye told me about the goat.

Fergal Did I tell yer about the storm?

Ruairi (*low*) Don't think so.

Fergal Hey?

Ruairi No: tell me about the storm.

Fergal (*announcing the story with a great deal of gravity in his voice*) I only went to Argentina by chance. It was my first voyage at the age of nineteen and it only came about as a matter of necessity.

Ruairi How far's Argentina?

Fergal Thousands of miles.

Ruairi Thousands of miles. See, this is what I'm sayin – how can ye think of that? Thousands of miles and millionaires . . . There must be an incredible freedom in the world, somewhere.

Fergal I heard last minute that this ship, *The Errant Son*, was sailing out, and I was in need of a sharp exit as I had some fellas after me life as a result of a terribly compromising romantic entanglement, that I'll tell yer about on another occasion. Anyhow, I beg meself a place on the crew and as I'm climbing on board this ship, waving te people as ye do, my eye catches on a pretty girl standing all alone. So I give her the wink and the nod like, and this lovely little thing blushes pink and blows me a kiss. So I'm thinking it was all a great laugh –

Ruairi How pretty was she?

Fergal Ye'd give her yer eyes just te look at her. But what I don't know yet, is that this pretty girl is only the fiancée of the famous old bastard of a boatswain, Ned Bannister, known fer workin men within an inch of their deaths. Anyhow, Mad Ned's seen this, and clearly made a note of it in his mind, 'cause every day I'm on that ship he makes a living hell. He has me up at dawn, cleaning and rigging and every other thing, all the day long mocking and taunting me, calling me an Irish dandy, calling me a thick Mick, saying I'm a toad of a man and I'll never survive at sea.

Ruairi Did ye batter him?

Fergal Ye know not te try and batter a man like Ned Bannister. Two feet across he was: two and a half feet when he was angry. So I kept my head down and thought he'd have te let up some time.

Ruairi But I bet he didn't.

Fergal He didn't; no. And when we arrive in Argey it's even worse. He has us all working in the heat loading cotton, sun up te sundown, and of course it's me who gets the worst of it, and nothing but insults in me ears te boot.

Ruairi How hot was it?

Fergal The skin was dripping off our shoulders. (*Beat.*) So this goes on an I'm about ready to lose me mind, till one day the lot of us set off in to the hills te collect more supplies. It's a beautiful country, Ruairi: eagles in the air and sand the colour of gold; but these hills were hard as hell itself te navigate, and we're starting te think Mad Ned might have led us off track, when suddenly, in a matter of a minute, a storm sets in.

Ruairi Bloody hell.

Fergal And I mean an electric storm like I pray to God you'll never witness. The sky shocked bright white as trees caught fire at a distance, deafening thunder, whipping rain and winds so powerful it was all we could do te find shelter in a nearby cave. Men are crying out fer mercy but this thing lasts for a good half-hour, then, sudden as it began, it stopped.

Ruairi Can that happen?

Fergal It happened. (*Beat.*) But now we've a new trial te face, as emerging from our little hole in the rock we see that the way we came is utterly transformed. A great tree that musta stood at forty feet has been dragged to the ground by the pitiless wind; its branches lying across our path in such a way as to trap us completely. Now first thing we do is we run at it one and all, fifty men, to try and shift it, but this thing is wider than ten men and even with all of us pushing, it doesn't give an inch. The men are getting desperate now but I'm shoutin out: 'Keep pushin, fellas! Don't give up,' and ye can imagine Mad Ned Bannister didn't much like me giving out orders, so he starts in on me as usual –

Ruairi The arl bastard.

Fergal He's sayin, 'Fergal Monahan, who are you te give these men advice when yer thin like a twig and thick like a tree?' And it all came out about his missus and how I thought I was Casanova giving her the eye, and how she wouldn't touch me with the end of her oldest shoe; but I'm trying not to listen, I'm thinking about the task at hand, I'm thinking about getting out of there alive. But then – (*He pauses for an intake of breath.*) I won't tell yer what he said next, as it's not fitting for a Christian man's ears, but it involved my mother and a goat.

Ruairi He never?

Fergal Now I don't remember much of what happened next 'cause I saw red in front of my eyes and nothing else, but I could hear his insults round and round me head and according to the others a look, almost divine, passed across my face, as I put every inch of my anger

40

into that tree, I shoved it with every red hot feeling in me, and the bloody thing moved.

Ruairi No!

Fergal Not far, but it moved. Forty foot of tree, ten men wide. I shifted it, just enough fer it te come loose in the earth, so when the other fellas all got behind it, the magnificent thing rolled off down that hill and right out of sight.

Ruairi What did Mad Ned say?

Fergal He never said a word to me again that wasn't polite.

Ruairi Too scared.

Fergal They were calling me Mad Fergal after that.

Ruairi I bet thee were! I bet thee carried ye back down that hill!

Fergal They did.

Ruairi I bet yer had more drinks than ye could handle that night!

Pause as Ruairi's excitement subsides and he notices Fergal watching him.

Fergal (*taking Ruairi's hand tightly*) Ruairi, ye'll listen to me, won't ye?

Ruairi Tell us the one about the giant bird of Lisbon.

Fergal Perhaps I've no more stories in me.

Ruairi Come on!

Fergal Perhaps I'm too much of an ache.

Ruairi Ye never are.

Fergal Ruairi –

Ruairi I love that bird.

Fergal Ye'll listen to me, won't ye? No one else will.

Ruairi Listen te what?

Fergal Promise me you'll listen when I need ye to.

Ruairi I promise.

Fergal I'm not mad. I'm old and sick but I'm not mad. Don't let them tell you I am.

Ruairi Okay, I won't.

Fergal You promise me?

Ruairi I promise. (*Beat.*) Tell me about the bird.

Fergal It was a really beautiful bird. Wings as wide as yer body's breadth. Saw it on the horizon as the boat drew in.

Ruairi resumes tapping his bottle. Lights down.

SCENE THREE: INDOLENCE

The following morning. Brynjar stands halfway up the stairs looking out into the court, not long dragged out of sleep, with his blanket wrapped round him. We hear a muffled argument with screams of animal aggression interjected from out in the court. Fergal is in a state of half-consciousness, coughing up the night's phlegm. He stirs and moans at intervals. Ruairi lies in his pile of rags, burying his head, suffering badly from his hangover. Niamh is woken by the noise. The whiskey bottle is now back on the table, but much is missing from it. She goes to the stairs, edging Brynjar out of the way to see what's happening.

Ruairi (*slowly; referring to the noise*) Jesus, is that Ma?

Niamh Who else?

A loud scream from the court. Brynjar moves away from the stairs in anger.

Ruairi What the bleedin hell's she doing?

Niamh Right now?

Brynjar (*to Niamh*) Come away. There are enough fools to gawp.

Niamh Right now she's draggin Mrs Olsen by the hair; shouting down her earhole.

Ruairi (*to himself, of his hangover*) My bastard head.

Brynjar (*to Niamh*) I told you to come away.

Niamh Ye maybe wanna get out there and protect yer lady wife?

Millie (*from off*) There's not one person in this court doesn't know yer talk shit, Jan Olsen!

Brynjar I think she'll manage.

Niamh Wouldn't want to dirty ye suit, yeah?

Ruairi Jesus, my head.

Niamh You know what it'll be, don't ye?

Brynjar Something and nothing; a squabble between birds.

Niamh Ye know it's not the first beating she's given on your account.

Brynjar I know it's the last.

Niamh You reckon, do ye? I'm not so sure.

Brynjar Niamh, *please*. Please, could you dress and go to work.

He sinks down into the chair with great weariness. The shouts in the court continue. Niamh eyes him for a moment.

Niamh Ye know what it'll be, Ruairi?

Ruairi I don't care –

Niamh Ye know the mouth Mrs Olsen's got on her –

Brynjar (*pointedly*) You must already be late for work, Niamh.

Niamh (*aimed at Ruairi, but performed for Brynjar*) Well, it's a fair assumption really. Anyone'd wonder looking at the two of them together.

Brynjar Or perhaps for your work, the hour is never too late.

Niamh I mean it just doesn't fit; him beside her; small wonder tongues wag.

Brynjar Stop this.

Niamh I mean, who wouldn't wonder? 'Why on earth would a fella on the rise like that hang about in there with that band of hopeless drunks?'

Brynjar You want me to give you an answer?

Niamh Mrs Olsen came up with her own answer.

Brynjar For you all is dark and difficult and suspicious, but you see for me it is easy. My answer to you is easy.

Niamh See Mrs Olsen's been shouting up and down the place that Ma drugs him. (*Laughing.*) She reckons she's been slipping something in ter his dinner for a year now.

Brynjar I love your mother: that's my answer.

Niamh What, her out there? That mad bitch?

Beat. We hear screams. Laughing.

They'll say worse about her now.

Brynjar It's this place. She'll be different –

Niamh And what's gonna change her, hey? *Love?* (*Beat.*) Your love?

Millie (*entering, shouting back into the court*) Yeah, go on and talk; yer good fer nothing else!

Brynjar Millie; the baby – You can't just –

Millie Don't worry; I didn't let her get near me. (*A beat as she takes in the room.*) Up, Ruairi!

Brynjar puts his head in his hands in frustration.

Niamh Ye tryna start a war round here? Ye'll have all four of them Olsen lads batterin our door in, next thing ye know.

Millie Bitch said I'm lying. (*To Brynjar.*) Did ye hear that?

Niamh Whole of Liverpool heard.

Millie Said I'm makin it up 'bout the job and us moving.

Brynjar It doesn't matter what she believes.

Millie She said she's never seen anyone get out of this court unless they've been kicked out, in her whole wrinkled old life. Talkin at me like I'm actin above meself . . .

Brynjar (*with more emphasis*) It doesn't matter what she believes.

Millie I said, then I'll be the first and you'll be eating your words for breakfast. (*Beat. To Brynjar.*) I mean she's wrong, isn't she? We're not dreaming here?

Brynjar Of course she's wrong.

45

Millie That's what I told her. (*Her eyes resting on Ruairi suddenly.*) Ruairi!

Ruairi moans and rolls in his bed. Millie goes to him and grabs his feet. She tries to pull him up out of the covers, but he bellows and frantically clings to them, cramming them around his head.

Get yerself in an earn yerself something.

Ruairi (*burrowing under the covers like a dog, only his legs showing*) I'm not going.

Millie Fer God's sake, I shouldn't be draggin yer up, yer nearly a man.

Ruairi (*from under the covers*) So let me alone.

Millie (*ripping the cover off him*) Oh. Oh right. Let's all just give up and drink, one an all, shall we? Give the gossips out there something else te say about us.

She throws herself down at the table beside Brynjar and takes a swig of the whiskey.

Niamh (*pre-emptively*) I'm in late today.

Millie Oh Jesus! How many lates is that?

Niamh A few.

Ruairi stands, shaking the covers off him, gaining his balance.

Millie (*noisily mashing banana for Fergal's breakfast; to Brynjar*) Ye'll have te make sure they don't decide they've made a mistake when ye get te this job. Be careful what ye say, ye know; make a good impression.

Brynjar Of course I will.

Millie Don't mention ye wife was married before.

Ruairi begins to play a single bass note repetitively on the piano.

Niamh So where did we come from, eh?

Millie Stay out of it.

Niamh There's no way any bugger'd believe he fathered *me*.

Millie And don't tell them I sell at the market. Ye know what half the girls who work St John's are; they'll think ye married a whore.

Brynjar Millie, you should calm down – the baby –

Millie nods and sits, breathing deliberately more slowly, continuing to mash the banana. For a brief moment there is relative quiet.

Millie What'll it look like, de ye think? I mean, how do we even get it? How do we even know who te talk to?

Brynjar We'll get there. I've told you –

Millie But how? People like us – how do we –?

Brynjar I have an address for a man I can call on. A landlord –

Millie Landlord where? What does he have?

Brynjar He has good places – Svein Torre at the Scandinavian hotel swears he is a trustworthy man –

Ruairi hits the bass note louder.

For goodness' sake, Ruairi –

Millie I mean, what do they actually look like, these places –?

Brynjar He said maybe Lime Street.

Millie Lime Street?

Brynjar The new places on Lime Street.

Millie We couldn't have one of them.

Brynjar We'll find out.

Millie We *couldn't*.

Brynjar Why couldn't we?

Millie You're saying we could?

Brynjar I'm saying we could, maybe –

Millie Oh my God! (*Beat.*) I've never really tried lookin into one. (*Beat.*) They have curtains there, don't they? I've seen they have curtains.

Niamh Ye can take the girl out the cellar . . .

Millie (*to Brynjar*) What's she mumbling at me?

Brynjar I don't know.

Millie (*to Brynjar*) I'll go te Simms after the market today. Shove him his money and tell him that's the last bit of rent he gets off me for this hole in the ground. Tell him to go stuff his coal up his arse 'cause our money'll buy no more of it for him.

Brynjar (*referring to the repetitive bass note*) Ruairi, please?

Millie And we'll have to go upstairs to it?

Brynjar I think so. Probably.

Millie And there'll be a sink?

Brynjar Of course.

Millie All that water.

Ruairi (*not turning from the piano, but directing at Millie*) De ye remember a day last spring, Mrs McTigue in here weeping?

Millie Do I what?

Ruairi Last spring, Nell McTigue in here: eyes shot red 'cause the bleedin council knocked the cellars in on Lime Street and her whole family had to be crammed across the way with Mrs Flannigan?

Millie I've reared a lunatic.

Ruairi Till they turned them out of there too for overcrowding.

Millie What of it?

Ruairi You with your arm on her shoulder, rantin and gnawin 'bout them shiftin us round like freight, turning us out like dogs?

Millie So what if I was?

Niamh He's sayin yer a two-faced cow.

Brynjar Those cellars were rotten. They were a danger.

Millie (*to Niamh*) I'm a *what*?

Niamh I'm not sayin it.

Ruairi Yer just walkin up and taking her home now?

Millie Council took her home.

Ruairi You stood there and said it was wrong. Wrong them knocking in our rooms te make new stuff we couldn't afford. I heard ye. Ye said it was wrong.

Millie It *was* wrong.

Ruairi So now yer gonna live in one of them things? What's new now except his bloody money?

Brynjar Those cellars were rotten with disease.

Ruairi (*to Brynjar*) We already know what side you're kickin for.

Millie Ye know who ye remind me of, Ruairi, propped up there shoutin the odds to everyone and no one? The bleedin ghost of yer bleedin Da.

> *Ruairi suddenly begins hammering out the tune to a rowdy pub song, 'Beer, Glorious Beer', on the piano, channelling all his anger, frustration and headache into it. Brynjar buries his head in his hands.*

Millie (*smiling in spite of herself*) Ruairi, come on, are ye mad now?

> *We hear the neighbours banging on the wall in appreciation, joining in singing sporadically. The baby begins to cry.*

Ruairi (*shouting to Brynjar*) You think you deserve more than most, Sildnes? You think you were born under a brighter star?

Brynjar Every man who can pull himself up and try deserves more.

Ruairi What does that mean?

Brynjar Every man can be something.

Ruairi Oh yeah, and what can I be?

Brynjar You can be – (*Beat.*)

Ruairi Yeah? Tell me. What can I be?

Brynjar (*beat*) I just want a quiet morning, that's all I want.

Ruairi Then go home, because there's nothing quiet here.

The baby's crying suddenly becomes a howl. Ruairi stops playing. The singing that has continued next door stops and we hear an anxious female voice. Pause.

Millie It was the same last time: babies went first.

Niamh Could be anything.

Millie The poor bitch lost two last time around. No bleedin justice –

Niamh Ma, the kid's wailing, not buried.

Brynjar (*quietly to Ruairi*) I am home.

Ruairi Eh?

Brynjar I am home.

Ruairi (*beat*) Then God help ye.

Ruairi slams the piano lid down and exits, grabbing his clothes and shoes. Brynjar begins hurriedly to gather up his things for work. Millie watches him, frightened.

Millie It's only 'cause he isn't working.

Brynjar He's young. He doesn't know what he hates and what he envies.

Millie Sometimes he's nothing but his father.

Niamh Because you're the Virgin Mary –

Millie (*approaching Niamh threateningly*) Niamh, I swear I'll take a hand te you –

Brynjar (*taking hold of Millie*) We'll have no more battles fought with hands. No more fighting in the streets –

Millie (*to Brynjar*) You didn't hear old Olsen talkin –

Brynjar We are not those people any more –

Niamh No, we're all of us transformed.

Brynjar (*pointedly*) Why don't you go to work, Niamh?

Niamh (*doing a mock-curtsy*) Whatever you say, Mr Sildnes.

Brynjar draws Millie aside to speak to her. Niamh throws on a shawl and, seeing that she is being ignored, exits defiantly.

Brynjar I don't know who you are when I see you acting like this.

Millie There's a certain way of surviving round here –

Brynjar You are not surviving any more.

Millie It's only *me* under a bit of anger –

Brynjar (*going to her*) Tell me what you'll do next time a woman in the court spits insults at you?

Millie (*beat*) Ye walk away from a row round here, they'll try anything on after –

Brynjar The men I will work for don't know about the courts or fights. They know women who only sit all day long in dresses –

Millie There's not much call fer that round here.

Brynjar I have been told that Mr Thompson once fired a man for screaming out a profanity when he stubbed his toe.

Millie People talk –

Brynjar It is said that once, at dinner, a bowl of steaming soup was spilt into his lap, and so gentlemanly was he that he didn't even flinch.

Millie What a waste of soup.

Brynjar It's you who talks of right impressions, Millie –

Millie So I don't fight.

Brynjar If it was ever known that you –

Millie It was only the gall of her –

Brynjar (*wearily*) Millie.

Millie So I won't fight.

Brynjar You'll hold your head up and walk on, yes?

Millie (*beat*) Yes.

He kisses her hard on the cheek. She hugs him quickly and picks up her basket and shawl.

Best get te that market while there's money left to make.

Brynjar You and I are starting again.

She holds his eye and smiles before exiting. The baby through the wall makes intermittent noises. Someone sings an inaudible nursery rhyme. Brynjar sits for a moment breathing in the relative quiet. He leans his head on his hands in weary thought. Lights down.

SCENE FOUR: IMPROVIDENCE

Early that afternoon. The flies are particularly bad at this time of day. We hear them more clearly. Pieces of half-entwined rope lie on the table beside a pile of extracted oakum. Fergal sits, propped up, his breathing worse but his eyes wide open and alert. Millie is at his side with a bucket of water and a sponge. During the following exchange she attempts to wash him, turning him in the bed with painful difficulty. He winces throughout.

Millie That baby's had the shits for three days now. Edna's been wandering the streets for a doctor.

Fergal She'll get *five* doctors; two days late, with notepad and pencil to take down the numbers.

Millie She's convinced it's the cholera.

Fergal You working yerself up over it does no one any favours.

Millie The air smells just the same as the last time round.

Fergal Calm yerself: think of yer own child.

Millie I *am*.

Fergal There's always been fever, Mill.

Millie Five dead on Lace Street, I heard.

Fergal Yer lookin pale –

Millie I'm fine.

Fergal You're old te be havin that child –

Millie I'm *fine*.

He cries out in pain as she turns him over roughly in the bed.

You'll see: same as five years back. Half the court gutted.

Fergal I'll not see.

Millie I'm not a kid now, Da; ye can't tell me stories that everything's fine. I know what's comin.

Fergal I'll not see 'cause I'll not survive another bout like that.

Millie (*rolling him over again, causing him to wince*) You'd survive the apocalypse.

Fergal Not so hard.

She takes no notice of this instruction.

Millie (*beat; she douses the sponge*) And Brynjar thinks we're charmed.

Fergal Maybe God's smiling on yer fer once.

Millie Down here? We barely get sunlight. (*Beat.*) The hopes he has fer this child. He has it climbing mountains and running the docks before it's out the womb.

Fergal He'll love it.

Millie He will that. And he'll love me for having it. He's got that pure heart, ye know, like no one's ever hurt him and everythin's just hope? People round here can't love like that –

Fergal He's a good man.

Millie Too good.

Fergal (*pointedly*) No.

Millie (*pauses in her task, her hand on her stomach*) I can't imagine the child, the way he talks about it: the things it'll have and be and do. It's like I'm giving birth to someone else's child, not mine. And what'll it think of me? This wonder child I'm gonna raise? What in the world'll it think of me?

Fergal It'll be you as much as it's him.

Millie (*beat; she resumes washing him roughly*) God help it then.

Fergal You spend all yer time convincing Brynjar he's no life with you, he might start believing yer.

Millie Spent fifteen years of my life with a man telling me I was nothing, Da. How'm I supposed to know what te do with someone telling me I can have everythin?

Fergal I cried the first time yer married, Mill. Not 'cause I was losing yer, but 'cause yer knew what kind of a man he was: ye knew what life'd be with him and ye married him all the same. I thought te myself, 'Did I raise my child te think so little of herself?'

Millie What's all this all of a sudden?

Fergal (*pause*) There was this time when ye were a little girl –

Millie If you start on one of yer stories I'm gonna walk outa this room –

Fergal It's a memory – a flickering – barely a story at all.

Millie (*sarcastic*) I'll bet.

Fergal There was this time when you were a tiny thing, 'bout three yer were. Back in Dublin, in Boyne Street, when yer ma was still living. We'd been out te the market together, and we're walking back through the streets hand in hand, when you see this doll in some toyshop window – one of those posh places that don't sell anything that doesn't have a frill on it. And I'm telling yer te hurry up, as ye ma'll have ye tea done, but you're transfixed by this thing: this doll with a white china face and these big green eyes and some sorta pink dress on, I think.

Millie You're telling me this is true?

Fergal This is true, I swear it. Te tell ye the truth the thing gave me the shudders, with those painted lips and eyelashes, but you thought she was the most beautiful thing ye'd ever looked on. Ye gave her a name: Silvie.

Millie I did not.

Fergal I'm telling ye: ye were in love with the thing. So much so that when I pulled yer away at last, ye howled

56

and cried and demanded all the way home and all the evening after that you had to have this doll. You couldn't live without her. And we had no more money then than you or I do now and I told yer so, many times. But fer days yer couldn't lift yer face off the floor fer wanting this bloody thing, till in the end yer mother pawned her good pair of shoes –

Millie Oh Da, fer a doll? Come on?

Fergal I'm telling yer, it meant so much to ye, she went ahead and got it for ye. Now, here's the thing –

Millie Who knew there'd be a twist?

Fergal A week later, I come in from working the docks te find pieces of this doll's face scattered all over the room, and you sat in the middle, not knowing what te do with yerself. Ye'd thrown the bloody thing te the floor in a fit of rage.

Millie Now that sounds more like me.

Fergal And of course I cursed you till the sun went down and came up again, but you only had one explanation for what ye'd done. Ye kept saying: 'It was too pretty, and it was always looking at me.' 'It was too pretty, and it was always looking at me.'

Millie (*beat*) I never did like dolls.

Fergal (*imploring*) Millie –

Millie I know what yer saying, Da.

Fergal I'm saying don't break this. (*Beat.*) Think more of yourself for me.

Lights down.

SCENE FIVE: INTEMPERANCE

*Late that night. The rain outside is thick but the
atmosphere is warm. A fire burns centre stage. A suit and
shirt now hang from the rafters centre stage, with shoes
positioned below and a hat above, to form the shape of
a man. There are now several bottles of beer scattered
about the room, some empty, some full or part full, the
whiskey bottle still taking pride of place in the centre of
the table. There are also a huge number of banana skins
strewn about, and Niamh and Brynjar still hold a banana
each. Fergal is propped up on his mattress, breathing
with great difficulty but somewhat revived by the beer
he drinks. Niamh and Millie sit on the floor, and during
the scene they distractedly pick oakum from the ropes.
Brynjar sits in the chair centre stage in a state of slightly
inebriated intensity. He scribbles a letter at intervals.
Through the wall we hear the accordion playing a
traditional jig to occasional singing and joyous chatter
and shouts. In amongst this we occasionally hear a baby
laughing.*

Millie Ye hear that laughter? That's like angels humming
in my ears –

Fergal The young thing'll live to a hundred.

Millie In there an hour ago, that baby was sitting up,
eatin, spitting: every which thing she coulda been doin.
Court born is what she is – tough as any one of us, may
God bless our hard little hearts! Te think the fear a minor
case of the shits has in us now.

> *Next door the accordion starts up, playing a jig. Millie
> and Fergal cheer instinctively, and Fergal thumps on
> the wall in appreciation*

The relief on that woman's face!

Niamh 'Smell of the air,' hey, Ma?

Millie Smells bad enough at the best of times, how'm I te say?

Fergal Doctor came by today with his notebook.

Millie And no news – Edna said – no news. Not a single death.

Niamh Not a one?

Millie (*pronouncing each word triumphantly*) Not a one.

Fergal He says, 'Any dead? Any diarrhoea?' I said, 'I could ask the same of you.'

Millie You didn't.

Fergal No.

Millie (*looking over his shoulder at his letter*) Where's Brynjar the American adventurer at today?

Niamh Probably wrestling with tigers; the hero that he is.

Brynjar (*lifting a banana from the table and holding it to the light from the fire*) I write to my father of bananas.

Niamh I'm sure he'll be riveted.

Brynjar He will marvel. We have nothing so modern as bananas in Norway. Sweet like sugar, filling like bread, it arrives from the tree wrapped clean and tidy. If a man had made the banana he would be a very great man. But man's greatness was not in the making. No: it was in the moving. *This* – (*Beat.*) is progress.

Niamh I'm almost scared to swallow.

Brynjar It is my papa's birthday today.

Fergal (*raising his bottle and drinking deeply*) As good a reason as any.

Millie (*to Fergal*) Like you need an excuse.

Fergal (*raising his bottle again*) To Brynjar's da!

Brynjar (*raising his banana*) My father is an old man!

Millie raises her bottle in assent.

Fergal Nothin so big as the sea te put between yerself an yer own, I know that much.

Brynjar He would not like to see me now.

Fergal But home's always where you started, hey? Always where you began.

Brynjar He'd never talk to me unless he was drunk, and then he would do nothing but talk. He'd tell me over and over: 'You are a good and sober Lutheran man. You are all that I am not.' One day he catches me drinking beer with my friends. He breaks down. He cries.

Fergal Right now, he'll be raising you a glass across the ocean.

Brynjar Poor Papa; when I picture him he is standing pointing out to sea: to America and my new life. (*Beat. He laughs coldly.*) A lifetime spent planning a voyage I never completed . . .

Millie (*lifting her bottle*) Here's to not getting to America.

Brynjar Sometimes as I walk through town, beggars at my elbows, pushed between racing wheels and feet, I close my eyes and I imagine the stillness of the mountains in Sunndalsøra, when the water was calm: the stillness of the air and of the land.

Millie I'd love te see a mountain.

Brynjar Then I am so glad to be far away inside the noise and rush. Then it is medicine to me. Then I know my home is where I stand.

Fergal You know I'm a rural man myself. Born in the fields.

Millie (*reacting to the absurdity of the statement*) Jesus.

Fergal Out near Omeath, 'fore the move te Dublin. We had a bit of land, I think . . . truth of it is I don't remember much. Just a lot of mud and sky, and that we had a dog and a goat. And the mountains of Mourne off in the distance. Just shapes.

Brynjar In Sunndalsøra the mountains are not like shapes; they are walls without doors. There might be something on the other side. There might be nothing. But between you and that place the world might as well lie.

Fergal There's always a bit of me feels I mighta belonged te the sky an the mud.

Niamh We've enough dirt here.

Fergal It was some kind of paradise as I remember it.

Millie I thought you didn't remember?

Fergal (*to Brynjar*) But it's clean there, hey? Ye've the clean air and the water?

Brynjar It's clean enough to drink.

Millie And ye've no disease now at all?

Brynjar Almost none now.

Millie God must love ye.

Brynjar Love us or forget us. Bless us or leave us be.

Millie (*recounting what he's told her before*) And ye've each a house made of wood, isn't that right?

Brynjar Small houses, yes – *hytte*: nothing grand, nothing high; nothing shouting of greatness like men build here.

Fergal A house each? And enough food?

Brynjar There were always fish in the sea . . .

Fergal All that dinner swimming past!

Brynjar I am a boy. My father walks in front of me with a spade in his hand, weary from digging.

Fergal Ye don't know yer born!

Brynjar I have something to say to him but with the mountains and the silence I cannot. I have something to say. But I can't get to it.

Fergal To live out there in all that air and sky and mud!

Brynjar May a boat never tempt me back to that space between the mountains.

Fergal raises his bottle with a cheer.

Millie Da, that wasn't a toast.

Fergal I thought we were in need of one.

Millie Ye've toasted everything in the bleeding room.

Brynjar A toast to my new suit!

Fergal We can't forget the suit.

Brynjar When I wear my new suit, men will listen!

Millie To your suit!

Fergal The suit.

Brynjar (*warmly, looking Millie in the eye*) To never getting to America.

Millie allows him a moment of affectionate eye contact. Ruairi enters at speed down the steps, so drunk and uncoordinated that he almost falls into the room. He makes a grab for Niamh, pulling her to her feet.

Niamh Jesus, get off me.

Ruairi I want a waltz with me sister, that's all. Come on, where's the song?

He goes to the wall through which we can still hear the accordion and bangs on it with his fist.

Louder!

The neighbours respond, hammering and shouting back and playing louder.

Fergal What's your celebration?

Ruairi Black Magic!

Millie My God, he's gone over to the devil.

Ruairi Brought Big Owen in a half-shilling!

Niamh It's a horse, Ma – what else?

Ruairi Truth be told I've drunk enough wine to kill a man.

Millie And enough to make an eejit of a boy.

Ruairi (*grabbing her in a dancing postion*) Give us some steps, Niamhy.

Niamh Leave off!

Millie If he's not ranting in anger he's ranting in madness.

Ruairi (*pushing Niamh round the room to the music*) You remember bein small and Da dragging us up, banging out a beat on the table – Grand-da up and battering the floorboards –

Fergal Now, *I* was a dancer.

By now she's dancing with him; allowing him to lead her trampling all over the room.

63

Niamh I remember Da making us show off for the neighbours, and you trampling all over me feet.

Millie (*scuttling out the way*) Jesus, you're like a two-headed beast!

Ruairi He spent it all! His whole half-shilling!

Millie The useless fool.

Ruairi Useless nothing – He bought the night for us – bought us a bit of light and heat and time – The lot of us singing in there in the warm – hangin on to each other like sailors in a storm –

Niamh Ye know what they did with the drunken sailor?

Ruairi It's a terrible shame yer not a man, Niamh. If ye were a man, ye could drink like a man, 'stead of crawling round in the dark in here.

He comes to a stop, exhausted, and lets Niamh go, falling back onto his pile of rags.

Niamh (*looking down at him*) It's all crawling, Ruairi, no matter where ye do it.

She settles on the floor near him.

Millie Half a shilling! I'll warrant yer Dan's wife won't be so pleased to wake up to a wasted husband instead of a joint a meat.

Ruairi (*rolling, clutching his stomach theatrically*) Oh Ma, ye shouldna mentioned meat!

Fergal I'll be tasting it all night now.

Ruairi Must be more than a month since I tasted a bit of meat . . . Bit of liver and onion . . .

Millie It was four weeks Friday – last time Brynjar got paid.

Fergal Nice bit of chicken or pork falling apart between me teeth.

Millie goes to Brynjar wearily and rests her head on his knee. He strokes her hair.

Ruairi Bacon. Liver and bacon fried up with onion.

Brynjar No more wanting and begging for you soon – We'll have meat at least once a week.

Ruairi Would ye leave off talking about meat!

Brynjar Our child will grow up with fine tastes.

Niamh Sure, it'll drink its milk from a golden cup.

Millie Gravy.

Ruairi moans in hunger at the thought.

I'd love a taste of gravy. A bit of gravy in a stew . . .

Ruairi (*to Niamh*) Dan Sharkey says ye spat at him in the street.

Niamh Serves him right – leering at me with that big black eye.

Ruairi He's half in love with ye, ye know? Reckons he's savin up te marry ye.

Niamh Ye can tell him he's better off saving hairs off his dog; he's half-bald at the age of eighteen.

Ruairi I told him I'll give him another eye te match if he keeps followin yer about.

Niamh They're like a bunch of apes, your mates.

Ruairi They call you the hardest girl in the north side, ye know? Finny was all in to takin the piss outa Dan – he says Niamh McLoughlin wouldn't wink at a fella if she had glass in her eye. (*He laughs.*) I said: too right and you're best to remember it.

Niamh smiles. Ruairi notices the ribbon poking out of her pocket. He tugs it out.

What's this?

Niamh Found it.

Ruairi Looks new enough.

Niamh I didn't nick it.

Ruairi No one's gonna see yer wearin it in yer pocket, anyhow.

He ties it clumsily in her hair.

Niamh Ta.

Ruairi (*standing grandiosely, addressing the room*) I saw that hall tonight; went right up close.

Millie Oh, here we go.

Ruairi The hall: have ye looked at it?

Millie Ye can't bleedin miss it, crouching up there on top of everything.

Ruairi The bastards left me. I took a piss up against sommat or other and the bastards all got off away and I was wanderin, and wonderin if I was walking the right way and then this thing, this great thing – and I never really looked at it I don't suppose. It was rainin on it and they've put them big lamps up and the thing was so . . . big. So I'm thinking I wanna see it, I wanna actually really see it and know what this thing's about, but ye know as I'm getting closer I'm getting smaller and smaller underneath the thing till all I see is rain runnin off stone. I can't see nothing.

Brynjar They made it to look like it was in Greece.

Ruairi (*incredulous*) Are things that big in Greece? (*Beat.*) I walked right up te the door and no one stopped me.

Millie Ye'll be getting yerself arrested, next thing.

Ruairi And I'm standing in front of this massive door – this *massive* door – like ten men on each other's shoulders could fit under it; and I'm standin there fer ages like I might just give it a push and walk inside. But I knew I couldn't; not even if it stood wide open. I'm reaching out te touch it 'cause it's like it might be imagination. Or someone else's imagination: nothing te do with me at all.

Millie Who says it's not? Perhaps I'll walk in there one day. Perhaps I'll walk round that corner and in through that big door, just like that. What's the difference? A few coins in yer pocket and a change of clothes?

Niamh (*deeply sarcastic*) Oh, is that the difference, Ma? Only that?

Millie Perhaps it is.

She goes to Niamh and rubs at the dirty marks on her face.

It's only dirt. Dirt rubs off.

Niamh And what's underneath?

Millie Do you not see we have a chance? We have a hope.

The revelry next door stops suddenly, as a woman lets out a grieved howl.

Millie The baby –

Fergal Aye.

Lights down.

Act Two

SCENE ONE: INSENSIBILITY

The following afternoon. Niamh enters hurriedly, checks that Fergal is sleeping. She takes money from her pocket and stuffs it in his mattress. Pulls liquorice out of another pocket and sits on the table chewing it triumphantly. After a short while she focuses in on the suit. She circles it, weighing up the possibilities. She picks up the whiskey bottle and unscrews the cap. Again she circles the suit, lifting the bottle playfully, toying with the idea of pouring it over the clothes. Millie appears in the doorway.

Millie Niamh!

Niamh (*jumping*) Shit! De yer have te scare me?

Millie Put that down.

Niamh (*doing so*) I was only having a joke with myself.

Millie There's a place for people who have jokes with themselves. Same place as for people who talk te themselves: the bleedin nut house.

Niamh I wouldna done it.

Millie Why ye even home?

Niamh Adler let me go.

Millie Yer fired?

Niamh I fainted. Swooned over a tank of boiling sugar.

Millie Yer not ill?

Niamh No Ma, it was only the heat.

Millie (*seeing the liquorice in her hand*) What's that?

Niamh (*sarcastic*) It's a letter from the Pope.

Millie I thought ye were past nickin sweets, Niamh – Brynjar'll go spare –

Niamh He'll probably break down and weep for my immorality –

Millie We all need to make a better reputation for ourselves –

Niamh I didn't steal it.

Millie So what; ye've been begging?

Niamh There's only one of us in this family in te grovelling –

Millie (*advancing on her*) Hey?

Niamh Every day of your life down on yer knees hoping and yearning: 'Rescue me, won't ye please!'

Millie runs at Niamh, who dodges out the way.

Ye might get to yer palace in the sky but you'll still be begging, Ma.

Millie launches herself at Niamh around the table. Fergal stirs. Just then we hear Brynjar humming happily as he approaches the stairway. Millie freezes, pulling herself up and trying to gain her composure.

Brynjar I've been to see it! Lime Street.

Millie Ye've been where?

Brynjar To our new home. A fine man with a moustache showed me round.

Millie And there's curtains?

Brynjar There are three rooms.

Millie Three! We can't afford that?

Brynjar We can.

Millie (*she laughs*) We can. Jesus alive!

Brynjar I told them we'll move in a month.

Millie When can I see it?

Brynjar When I'm first paid, we'll go straight there.

Millie And they won't give it away?

Brynjar shakes his head. He goes to Fergal and shakes him awake.

Da! Da! Ye hear this? We've a new place!

Fergal starts awake, calling out in surprise.

Fergal What? What now? What's happened?

Niamh takes the whiskey from the table and swigs from it.

Millie We've a place, Da! On Lime Street.

Fergal (*still recovering from his disorientation*) Ye could have told me when I woke.

Millie Three rooms. De ye hear me? Three rooms!

Fergal I hear!

Niamh goes to the piano and quietly begins to play the tune to 'The Mountains of Mourne'.

Brynjar There's a sink there, too – clean water whenever we need it.

Millie A sink, Da!

Fergal I'm right here.

Millie Can ye believe it, though? I'll wash yer till yer a prune – wash ten years off yer.

Fergal I haven't been out of this room in two years, Mill.

Millie That's because ye've had nowhere better to go. (*To Niamh.*) Stop yer miserable tunes when I'm tryna celebrate: ye'll have us all hangin ourselves.

Brynjar Why are you not at the refinery?

Millie Says she was too sick te work.

Brynjar (*challenging her*) Are you sick, Niamh?

Niamh Are you worried for my health, Mr Sildnes?

Millie Twelve months ye've lived with him, ye can't even give him his Christian name?

Brynjar You don't look sick.

Millie She's fine.

Niamh My da used to play this tune. He'd have me sat up on his knee; jog me up and down in time.

Millie That was me.

Niamh What was you?

Millie Your da never touched the thing. He pawned the clothes off your backs to buy it and then never touched it once.

Niamh (*stopping playing*) Don't try an tell me that, I remember –

Millie (*with emphasis*) He never played the thing. I should get rid of it.

Niamh You won't.

Millie Sits there reminding me of all his worst qualities.

Brynjar We'll get a new one.

Niamh We won't have a bleedin new one! It's my da's piano.

Millie It was my knee you sat on.

Niamh I remember his hands. I remember the red round his knuckles when he pressed the keys.

Brynjar I have to go back to work. I only came to tell you the good news.

Niamh (*to Brynjar*) How'd ye not laugh at her?

Brynjar You laugh enough for everyone.

Niamh He'd a laughed at you, Ma, you know that? (*Pointing.*) He'd have sat in that chair and pissed himself laughing at the pretence of you now.

Millie Who's pretending?

Brynjar There's space for you in Lime Street, Niamh. You'll sleep with a bed beneath you.

Niamh But I can't pretend, see. I can't pretend Mr Sildnes's little story is coming true.

Brynjar *Always*, I tell the truth.

Niamh You *think* you do.

She turns away and resumes playing.

Millie Don't listen to her. We've a new home.

Brynjar (*to Niamh*) I don't understand you.

Millie (*pulling him aside*) Nobody understands her. There is no understanding her. (*Kissing him.*) You get back to work now 'fore they miss ye.

Brynjar (*to Niamh*) You remind me of a cat I had as a boy.

Niamh (*turning to him, ceasing her music*) I *what*?

Brynjar A cat I found in a hole beneath our home; beaten. Boys had thought it was fun to beat her with stones. I took her inside and I kept her for years, but always when I raised my hand to stroke her, she cowered. She could not believe that the world had any kindness left for her.

Niamh (*beat*) Stories, Mr Sildnes; you're great at those.

Brynjar (*kissing Millie on the cheek*) I'm going.

Millie (*calling him back*) Come here.

She goes to him and kisses him again.

We have a new home.

He nods and they hug, all the while Millie's eyes fixed on the back of Niamh's head.

Brynjar We have a new home.

He exits. A moment, and then in a sudden vindictive movement Millie picks up the sponge doused in rainwater from the bucket and throws it at Niamh's head, soaking her and causing her to scream.

Millie You're a wicked thing, Niamh McLoughlin.

Niamh He'll leave ye, Ma. I'm telling ye –

Millie (*picks up her basket of oakum and bustles towards the door*) If you're here ye'll wash and feed yer grand-da and I'll earn us the food to eat today.

Niamh Did ye hear me?

Millie I'll not row with yer.

Niamh Yer were all set te tear me eyes out a minute ago.

Millie Ye can have a go at that rope an all when yer done.

Niamh Ye think those people'll want yer, Ma? Ye think ye can just throw on a new dress an they won't know where ye've been?

Millie (*as she disappears out of the door*) If you want a fight, go find one in the street.

Niamh (*shouting after her*) Too good te raise a hand to me now, are ye? Too much of a lady?

Pause as Niamh stands, shaking the water off her.

Bitch!

Fergal You pushed for it.

Niamh If she won't hear truth –

Fergal No one can hear you fer all yer talking.

Niamh He'll leave her. Course he'll leave her.

Fergal Give him a chance 'fore you chase him off.

Niamh Can yer honestly imagine her mixed in with that lot in Lime Street?

Fergal You and your ma are just the same, Niamh –

Niamh Playin bleedin dress-up and strainin te keep her back straight.

Fergal Clinging on to anything of use that floats by.

Niamh What does that mean?

Fergal I thought fer a while I might be shitting currency. Every time I woke up there were more notes in me bed.

Niamh (*beat*) You threatening me?

Fergal Put your bleedin claws away for once, girl. Ease up on her, is all I'm saying.

Niamh In six years I never saw her cry for my da. Not in six years. Not once.

Fergal Your mother hasn't cried since she was too small to know what crying was. Crack her open, the sea'd flood out, all the tears she's swallowed.

Niamh Let her drown in them.

Lights down.

SCENE TWO: INELOQUENCE

Early that evening. Ruairi plays a jig on the piano one handed, the now half-empty whiskey bottle in the other hand. Fergal is propped up on pillows in bed, breathing with even more difficulty. Ruairi begins to make up words to the tune. He has had a bit to drink but is still totally coherent.

Ruairi
My sister went a-walking, walking with a Mick,
Catch her down the alleyway, attending to his –

Fergal Oy!

Ruairi
My ma went out a-walking, walking on the dock,
My ma went for a friendly walk with a filthy foreign –

Fergal Ruairi! Great as it is to see yer in better spirits –

Ruairi I should curb my language.

Fergal You should curb somethin.

Ruairi There's a ship in. I saw it. Sugar, I reckon.

Fergal Ye sure?

Ruairi Own eyes – saw it. . . . be down there bright an

75

early, front of the line, which is why I'm not allowing myself to become too liquored.

Fergal (*facetious*) I *was* wonderin at your sobriety.

Ruairi There I'll be 'morra night, lying back drunk with effort.

Fergal Numb, and breathless and grateful.

Ruairi Ups and downs is a man's life.

Fergal It's no life.

Ruairi (*beat*) Y'ever go to that Norway?

Fergal Sweden, nearby, 's where we'd make runs for iron. Fell in love there.

Ruairi Yeah?

Fergal This is before ye grandmother.

Ruairi I wouldn't judge ye.

Fergal Well, it was. (*Beat.*) She came at me on skis. First time I saw her, would ye believe that?

Ruairi What's skis?

Fergal A flat bit of wood on each foot so's ye'd slide through the snow.

Ruairi Fast like?

Fergal Like a bat in the rafters.

Ruairi How much snow?

Fergal Everywhere – all as ye could see, and not thin and wet like here, thick and dry like a blanket – but freezing cold. (*Beat.*) Now this girl, Ana, she'd ski down each day –

Ruairi Brilliant.

Fergal Bringin me and the guys bits and pieces of food. No English, so it was only smiles and nods an that, but I was fallin for that smile and nod so fast – Anyhow, the last day we're there I decide to go walkin alone – last look at the place, and I'm lookin up admirin this cliff face – 'cause the water ye know it freezes as it falls, it's so cold –

Ruairi No!

Fergal I swear it does – in points: icicles.

Ruairi Icicles.

Fergal Big enough te slice through yer; hanging from the rock. Now as I'm lookin up, perhaps it's a sunny day far up on this mountaintop, perhaps it's someone messin about, or only God sending me a warning, but one of these icicles comes rocketing down towards me, and I mean from a hundred feet so fast I can't hardly have time te see it – straight through my leg.

Ruairi Jesus!

Fergal Through my calf, and pinnin me te the ground.

Ruairi No.

Fergal I swear and I'm screaming – I'm praying, I'm calling, I'm thinking I'm dead, and there she comes swooping over the hill like a bird – she's tearing down the landscape to me, and I'm slippin in and out of sleep the state I'm in, but she's there by my leg, and ye know what she does? She takes off her hat and gloves and strips right down to her vest.

Ruairi At a time like this?

Fergal And with the warmth of her body, pinned against me, she melts this thing, she holds this icicle until there is no icicle and she's only holding me. Ana.

Ruairi Yer a lucky bastard.

Fergal Couldn't walk on the leg fer a month or more.

Ruairi Lucky bastard.

Fergal These things happen out in the world.

Ruairi And she was in almost nothin in the snow?

Fergal Yer not trapped here, Ruairi.

Ruairi And wet through, I suppose.

Fergal I want you to go, Ruairi. Because I think if ye don't ye'll end up dead, or killin someone or at least just like yer father.

Ruairi (*pause*) We all end up dead, Grand-da.

Fergal Some of us live first.

Ruairi There's no way they'll let a thick bastard like me on a ship to Sweden or Lisbon or any other place. I'd be giving a bad impression and everything. Handful of times Ma kicked me te the school I couldn't get past writing my name. The nuns'd all be on at me that it was easy an a monkey could do it an all the letters always came out backwards and inside out. They'd say I could go bang the board duster 'cause I had a spectacular kind of stupid. (*Drinks from the bottle.*) Ye think men like me are sailors?

Fergal Ye don't need to be a sailor to sail.

Ruairi I've no money.

Fergal So *find* the money. Any way ye can. (*Beat.*) Perhaps you and I could both get out of here one way or another.

Ruairi Both of us?

Fergal I'm lost in this body, Ruairi.

Ruairi Shut up.

Fergal Ye'll help me, won't ye? Ye'll let me go?

Ruairi Don't ask me that.

Fergal I can have *that*, can't I?

Ruairi No.

Fergal Why de ye think I tell ye these stories? We can both find a little freedom.

Ruairi I'm not like you. I'm not a brave man. I'm not a clever man. I can't even say what I mean.

Fergal All's I could ever do was talk, Ruairi. Talked all my life, told tales, talked to merchantmen who told me their tales of other places, other lives, and every time I spoke those stories they became a bit more mine. A bit more part of me. I never went anywhere, Ruairi. I never did, because I'm not like *you*. (*Beat.*) Ye'll let me go, won't ye, Ruairi? No one else will.

Ruairi (*pause*) Aye. I will if ye want it.

Fergal grips Ruairi's hand.

Tell me a story.

Fergal Ruairi –

Ruairi Tell me a story.

Fergal is unable to. Ruairi resumes his one-handed gig, this time more slowly.

SCENE THREE: VIOLENCE

The following day. Late afternoon. Fergal lies in bed, semi-conscious and breathing with incredible difficulty. Ruairi sits in a chair on the opposite side of the room, watching him, leaning back on his chair so that it bangs rhythmically against the wall. Millie enters, highly

79

agitated. Again she has made an effort to tidy her hair and clothes. Throughout much of her speech to Fergal, her arm is over her stomach, protectively.

Millie (*to Fergal*) I saw it, Da. I stood in it. Just stood feeling like someone was gonna burst in and throw me out at any moment.

Ruairi Ma, I need te speak te ye.

Millie (*starting, surprised to see him*) Did they give ye no work on that cotton load?

Ruairi I didn't go.

Millie Ye didn't *what?*

Ruairi Ma, I've gotta speak te ye.

Millie All I hear of ye's there's no work!

Ruairi I couldn't go.

Millie I can't even talk te yer any more, Ruairi, 'cause I'm too low and disappointed with yer.

She goes to the bucket of rainwater and starts to wash her face again as she speaks.

Ruairi Ma, Grand-da's been talking at me –

Millie Ye shoulda seen the state of it, Da: the clean of it – the white empty feckin clean and bare space of it with light comin in off everythin.

Ruairi Ma –

Millie (*to Fergal*) Three bare rooms. Three times this place. And all as I'm thinking is what do I put in it? What in the world do I have to put in it?

Ruairi He can't hear ye, Ma.

Millie Don't speak te me, Ruairi, because I've no ears for ye.

Ruairi Ma, he's –

Millie (*to Fergal, continuing to scrub her face*) Brynjar's back yakkin te some German fella from the insurance place with gold glintin in his cuffs and a watch fallin out his pocket –

Ruairi He's been sayin things, Ma –

Millie He didn't look at me. He didn't suppose Brynjar was walkin with *me*. (*Beat.*) Da?

> *Brynjar enters, smiling. He bangs down a wrapped-up piece of meat and some bread.*

Brynjar Food for the body.

> *And then a music box.*

Food for the spirit. (*Aiming his words at Fergal but not looking at him.*) The men at my work had a 'goodbye' collection for me.

Millie (*to Fergal*) Ye imagine that? Rich fellas dippin into their pockets for us.

Ruairi He can't hear ye.

Millie I said, 'No way you're spending that money on a piece of nothing like a music box' –

Brynjar But I say, 'You are a lady now and ladies have luxuries.'

Ruairi What do you need it for?

Millie It plays a tune.

Ruairi (*to Millie*) I'll play yer a tune.

Brynjar It's a luxury! (*Starting the music box.*) It's me saying I love your mother.

Ruairi stares at him blankly. He bends down and speaks to Millie's belly:

Jeg elsker deg, lille Sildnes.

She laughs as he puts his arms around her. Fergal splutters, coughs. To Millie now:

Du er min skatt. Du er den eneste for meg.

Millie (*joking, pretending she understands him*) Absolutely not, what kind of girl de ye think I am?

Brynjar spins her round, forcing her to waltz to the music. Shouting to Fergal, still dancing:

Y'okay, Da?

Ruairi He's not okay.

Millie Just you wait'll I get you in a nice clean, soft bed in Lime Street. Wash yer in a bath of hot, clean water. Wash ten years off ye.

Ruairi He can't hear ye.

Millie stops and looks over at her father.

Millie Da?

Niamh bursts in, distressed, trying to hold back tears and even more upset to see a room full of people to greet her. She tries to turn to leave again.

Millie Niamh?

Niamh It's nothin. Don't look at me.

Ruairi (*jumping up*) Someone's belted ye?

Millie (*grabbing hold of her*) Who hit ye? Who hit ye?

Niamh No one. It's nothin.

Millie Niamh!

Brynjar Tell me who did this.

Niamh He fired me.

Millie Adler?

Niamh Yeah, course Adler.

Ruairi And hit ye?

Millie Why'd he fire ye?

Niamh I – (*Catching her breath through tears.*) I – (*Beat.*) He said I stole from him. I didn't. It's just . . . nothin –

Ruairi Then he hit ye?

Niamh Yeah.

Ruairi For stealin when ye never?

Niamh Yeah.

Ruairi It's always the bastard same, these bastards. Something missing and it's a Mick, it's always a Mick, isn't it? Bastard!

Brynjar Calm down.

Ruairi I won't!

Brynjar We need to think about this.

Ruairi We need to go round there and beat him like he was a little boy.

Brynjar No!

Ruairi Does he think he can just –?

Niamh Just forget it.

Ruairi Niamh, they think they can do anything to us!

Brynjar Sit down and we'll think about it.

Ruairi I'm going over there.

Brynjar Not in that anger you're not!

Ruairi Can't even speak English, telling me what to do?

Brynjar Sit down!

Ruairi I'm going over there.

Brynjar Millie, say to him.

Millie (*beat; to Ruairi*) I'm coming with ye.

Brynjar Millie!

Niamh I don't want ye goin over!

Fergal gasps for breath. Taking this in, Ruairi exits with a war cry. Millie starts after him.

Brynjar Millie.

Millie Ye want him te go alone?

Millie exits after Ruairi. The music box continues to tinkle. Niamh sits at the table, staring ahead of her as if transfixed. Brynjar stands watching her, not knowing what to do. She bangs the table with her hands suddenly.

Niamh *Shit.*

He puts a hand awkwardly on her shoulder. She shrugs him off.

Don't touch me.

Brynjar You haven't many friends left, Niamh. If I were you I'd be polite.

Niamh And you're my friend?

Brynjar Of course I am.

Niamh You're my friend if I'm *polite*: there's always a deal with you.

Brynjar I've protected you –

Niamh From what?

Brynjar You tell me the truth of why he hit you –

Niamh I'm gonna be out, I know *that*. She'll have me out. (*Touching her face.*) It bleedin hurts, the bastard –

Brynjar You tell me –

Niamh Ye don't wanna know.

Brynjar I already know: I want you to say it.

Niamh His wife found out what we'd been doing. She took it out on him. He took it out on me. Ye gonna make that nice and tidy and respectable?

Brynjar I'll speak to Millie –

Niamh *Why?* Why would ye do that?

Brynjar I want to be able to help –

Niamh You wanna clean us all up and clear us all away –

Brynjar And why not? Why can't I want you to be better?

Niamh You want us *good*. You want us *decent*, and we're not what we should be fer ye, Mr Sildnes. We're not that.

Brynjar So I'll make you that. I'll give you that.

Niamh We're not grateful, we're not humble and you're not our Lord and Saviour, so why not go off an find someone else te pity?

Brynjar And where would you be if I left?

Niamh 'I wanna help. I wanna light up the room fer yus. I wanna be the one who's needed and listened to 'cause Papa was always diggin.'

Brynjar I am your last friend in this world. When they come back through that door, knowing what you've done, you will have no one but me.

Niamh Why keep beatin yer head against a brick wall, Sildnes? Even a donkey knows to stop when it hurts.

Brynjar It has hurt for a year, Niamh, but I'm still here, because I am a good man, a good husband, and soon I'll be a good father, and you are just an angry little girl.

Niamh You wanna father me? What shall we do, shall I sit on your knee, scratch your back, tell ye how I spent my day? Well I'll tell ye shall I, how I spent my bleedin day?

Ruairi enters at the doorway suddenly.

Ruairi Why not tell me, Niamh, hey?

She looks at him, frightened.

I'd be very interested. 'Cause ye see Mrs Adler's out on Stanley Street shouting off an *old*, *old* tale about an Irish whore crawling all over her husband.

Niamh and Ruairi look at each other for a moment.

Give me a reason not to believe it. *Please.* Niamh, give me a reason.

Pause.

Niamh Y'understand I need to look after myself.

Ruairi runs at her, but Brynjar immediately gets in the middle. Instead of grabbing Niamh, Ruairi grabs Brynjar and forces him to the floor, clutching his clothing and shouting close to his face.

Ruairi Just low aren't we, eh? So fucking low. You disgusted by us, Viking? Ye hate the stink of us? Comin over here and makin me feel like shit? You think you have that right? Because we are shit? Because we *are* shit.

In a sudden surge of aggression, Brynjar rolls Ruairi over and escapes his grasp, pinning him to the floor. He bangs his head twice against the ground.

Brynjar You don't shout in my face! You don't shout in my face! You shout at the ships or the water or the air or the men who won't give you work or the age that kills your grandfather or the man who has been having your sister! You don't come to me and shout in my face!

Surprised by himself, he lets go of Ruairi and walks away, almost frightened. Ruairi remains lying on the ground. Long pause.

Ruairi Ye know, from the day I could think all as I wanted was te get big enough te kill him. Ye know that? Te kill my da for all he did te us, so I could be man in this place – make it better for her, and then the stupid bastard goes and gets drowned, and you . . . (*He pulls himself up.*)

Brynjar You're a child, Ruairi –

Ruairi *You* . . .

He staggers away into the room. He goes as if to leave but instead grabs hold of the rotten piano and putting all his weight behind it pushes it crashing to the floor. The shock of this wakes Fergal, who sits spluttering and gasping violently. Niamh goes to him and pulls him up in the bed, banging him hard on the back until he regains his breath and falls back into restless half-consciousness. The sound of the piano rings out. Brynjar walks slowly towards the door.

Niamh Go on, leave. I've been waiting to see that all year! I only wish Ma'd seen it coming as clearly.

He looks at her blankly a moment, then exits. The music box finally stops. Muffled voices are heard next door. Niamh pauses a moment, then starts frantically pulling together the few bits of rags and tiny objects in the room that might be hers, throwing them on a shawl. She goes to Fergal's mattress and pulls out money, hiding it in her clothes. Ruairi only now turns from looking at the remains of the piano. He sees this.

Ruairi Whore's money?

Niamh Grow up, Ruairi.

Ruairi Like we weren't low enough already.

Niamh Don't know 'bout you but I haven't been sat round waitin for a fool's dream te carry us outa here: I've made my own plans.

Ruairi goes over and clutches the arm of the suit, almost speaking to it.

Ruairi It'll be all round The Grapes. They'll all be sayin it and laughin. Ye had te take away me last bit of peace?

Niamh Funny enough, ye never crossed me mind.

Ruairi Everyone else's sister's up some alleyway with some fella every other night, but not mine; not Niamh. She's above all that.

Niamh You're right there: I'm above getting knocked up by some penniless no one who tells me he's in love; spend the rest of me life trippin over kids in a cellar room, scratching along like Ma. I'm so far above that.

Ruairi We're above nothing now.

Niamh Ye can't get lower than low, Ruairi; it's all the same thing. I'm not like Ma: I know what I am and I know what I've got but if I thought I'd never have anything better I'd lay down and die right now.

Ruairi Maybe I'll walk into that pub with a pocket full of cash and buy everyone a drink and laugh. I'll laugh like I'm not even bothered. Like I'm not bothered about anything.

Niamh What cash? Yer not havin my money.

Ruairi (*addressing the suit that still hangs in the shape of a man*) Shall I buy yer a drink, mate? (*Beat.*) No? Well, maybe you could buy me one. (*Taking the jacket and trousers from the hanger.*) Maybe ye could buy me a few.

Niamh (*realising his plan*) She'll go spare!

Ruairi Pawn shop'll still be open, yeah?

Niamh Ruairi, she'll go mental fer a week!

Ruairi We've all gotta look after ourselves, Niamh. You stick with what ye know.

Niamh Ruairi, don't, hey? Stay here with me, hah? For when Ma gets back?

Ruairi (*grabbing the suit jacket and trousers, leaving shirt, shoes and hat*) Ye know, there's no bridge across. Ye mighta got to see inside his big house – mighta got a feel of notes in yer pocket – got fed proper food and filled up with posh drink, but yer dreamin as much as Ma if yer ever think any of that'll belong te yer. There's no bridge across.

> *He exits with the clothes. Niamh stands, stunned. After a few moments, she collects up her things and heads for the door. Millie appears in the doorway, forcing her back into the room as she walks towards her, without looking at her. Niamh watches, frightened, as Millie goes to the bucket of rainwater and again washes her face, this time furiously. Niamh stands ready for a fight. Getting no response, she begins to pace the room, kicking her feet into the table, chair,*

bucket, remains of the piano as she passes them. At length, Niamh's fury building, she positions herself directly in front of Millie. Pause.

Niamh So what, ye can't see me now?

Millie I can see ye. I just don't want to look at ye.

Niamh If yer gonna tell me te get out just go ahead and say it.

Millie Where's Brynjar?

Niamh He battered Ruairi.

Millie What'd he do?

Niamh Battered Brynjar a bit, battered the piano a bit, had off.

Millie (*under her breath*) Jesus.

Niamh Think he saw us tonight, Ma. First time fer everything. Think he saw that shit raises shit and I think he's gone.

Millie Why de ye do it?

Niamh He was pushin money on me. Girls at the refinery started hatin me for the fact that he'd picked me. (*Beat.*) I liked that.

Millie I'm talking about Brynjar.

Niamh Hey?

Millie Why de ye do it?

Niamh Do what?

Millie (*not looking up from her work*) I will have him, whatever scene you cause, I will have this, in spite of the both of you. If you want to live like your father, so frightened of change you spit on anything pointing towards it, then go ahead, but I won't give birth to another child in a hole in the ground.

Niamh But it was good enough fer us?

Millie No, it wasn't, Niamh. It was never good enough for anyone.

Niamh I'm takin my money.

Millie I'm sure y'are.

Niamh So I'll go? (*Beat.*) Tell me if ye want me te go, I'll go!

Millie (*looking up at her*) Ye want me te tell ye te *stay*? Of course ye'll bloody stay! What else have ye got? A few quid? Grow up.

Niamh I've more than a few quid.

Millie And what'll that buy yer? And where'll ye go next time ye pockets run dry?

Niamh watches her a moment, infuriated by her lack of response. She takes Brynjar's hat from its position on top of the hanger and places it on her head.

Niamh Musta thought he could do without the hat.

Millie Hey? (*Swinging round to look at her at last.*) Where's his suit?

Niamh He took it, didn't he? I told yer, he's gone. He's staying gone.

Millie (*beat*) Look, I've had enough of the filth you spread fer one day –

Niamh Look fer yerself! (*Beat.*) He took his new suit and went off te find a better version of us, to match a better version of him.

Millie No.

Niamh Looks that way though, doesn't it, Ma? I told yer. I tried to say loads of times. He was always gonna do this. He was never gonna walk in te his new life draggin a bunch of drunks behind him.

Millie He loves me.

Niamh We don't suit him. You don't suit him. None of us'd look right out of this place.

Millie (*rises, looking around*) Ye've hidden it somewhere.

Niamh What *we* are, Ma, ye can't just wash off in a new bath. It's in the way we talk and breathe and move. They see it in us and they don't like it.

Millie (*putting her hand to her stomach*) He wouldn't just go.

> *Niamh makes a gesture as if to say: judge for yourself. Pause as Millie stands, overcome by this possibility. She takes the shirt that remains on the hanger and looks at it without seeing it. To Niamh:*

This is you. This is Ruairi and you. I could have pretended. I could have worked out how they walked and breathed and spoke.

Niamh But it woulda never looked quite right, and they'd have always seen ye trying.

> *Beat, as Millie attempts to control her anger.*

Millie Get out of my sight before I hurt ye.

Niamh It's him ye should be hating!

Millie This is what ye were waiting for, wasn't it? Me te tell ye te leave? Well, get going then.

Niamh Ma –

Millie (*turning her body sharply away so she has her back to her*) I don't wanna see yer fer a while, Niamh.

Niamh hovers as if to give a clever reply but, met only with her mother's turned back, exits. Millie remains where she is for a few moments before letting out an angry scream and tearing at the shirt in her hands, ripping it viciously into pieces. Brynjar appears in the doorway.

Brynjar I told you: 'Don't fight with your hands.'

Beat. Millie turns, surprised, the remains of the shirt in her hands. Seeing this:

You wish to see me in pieces?

Millie I thought I'd lost ye –

Brynjar Where's my suit?

Millie Niamh told me you took it.

Brynjar (*laughs*) She likes to lie. You may have noticed.

Millie Whatever they said te you, ye know – Whatever Ruairi did –

Brynjar I don't care what they did.

Millie They're only kids still –

Brynjar Mr Thompson takes a walk with his wife most evenings.

Millie What about it?

Brynjar I know this because I saw him just now and he told me there is no longer a job for me.

Millie He can't do that.

Brynjar He saw you. He saw my wife fighting in the street.

Millie Mrs Adler? That was barely a fight.

Brynjar I had made something. I had made something from nothing.

Millie So you'll speak to the guy. Ye'll sort the thing out –

Brynjar I ask you one thing.

Millie She was making a spectacle of me in front of the whole world – shouting about how the whole race of the Irish are nothing but muck. She said we're all cursed: angels at home and whores abroad –

Brynjar I think perhaps Niamh said one thing which was true.

Millie What? What did she say?

Brynjar She said that all of you are not what you should be for me.

Millie Brynjar – (*Beat.*) Brynjar, we've a baby here –

Brynjar I was to be a gentleman, Millie. I chased him down the street. I threw myself in front of him – all the people staring – I begged him –

Millie Ye'll speak te him again. Tomorra he'll feel different – We can put this right –

Brynjar No. No, we can't.

Millie He can't just do that. He can't just take it all away.

Brynjar You took it, Millie. You did it.

Millie looks at him, searching for the right words to solve this. He walks out slowly. Lights down.

SCENE FOUR: UNCLEANLINESS

That night. Ruairi stands over Fergal's bed, holding a pillow. He has his suit on and also a hat and coat. It is raining and the leak from the ceiling has become a steady stream, making the bucket below overflow. Fergal

94

breathes painfully now, but is barely conscious. Next door they sing a funeral hymn. After a time, Ruairi joins in quietly.

Abide with me, fast falls the eventide;
The darkness deepens, Lord with me abide!
When other helpers fail and comforts flee,
Help of the helpless, O abide with me.

I fear no foe with Thee at hand to bless;
Ills have no weight, and tears no bitterness.
Where is death's sting? Where, grave, thy victory?
I triumph still, if Thou abide with me.

Swift to its close ebbs out life's little day;
Earth's joys grow dim, its glories pass away;
Change and decay in all around I see;
O Thou who changest not, abide with me.

During the final verse, Ruairi presses the pillow down onto Fergal's face and smothers him, still singing to control his emotion. Fergal barely reacts but when he is absolutely still Ruairi kisses his forehead and, replacing the pillow, covers his face with the sheet.

Ruairi Sail away, Grand-da.

He takes out several notes, looks at them and replaces them in his pocket. He goes to exit, but Millie enters, stumbling through the door, massively drunk, falling into him to steady herself.

Millie Ruairi!

She tries to hug him, putting too much of her weight on him so he nearly falls.

Little Ruairi.

Ruairi (*trying to push past her*) Ma, I have te –

Millie Ye weren't always so rough te me. (*He stops.*)

95

Tiny baby – I called you a gift an a blessing. I did. Always quiet an always smiling. I'd think ye were dead ye were so quiet. And comin after yer sister ye were double the gift – 'cause oo hoooh she'd scream! Throw up everything. Never thought she'd live, not even keeping milk in her, but I didn't know then she had the bleedin devil incarnate living in her belly, keeping her on like a little feckin firefly. (*Beat.*) Was always my thought ye da only hit ye 'cause ye looked liked me. Was only me he was getting at.

Ruairi I can't be here, Ma.

Millie He thinks we're plants! Ye know that? Brynjar. He thinks we need watering and warm, and whatever sunshine he can buy. Well, he can piss off and stay gone. I'm no man's plant. (*Beat.*) Ye think he's coming back, Ruairi?

Ruairi I don't think anything.

Millie He saw us all of a sudden: not plants but animals. He doesn't know how to keep animals warm – ye know?

Ruairi I don't know anything.

Millie (*beat*) I bleedin love him. I do. Ye won't want to hear it, 'cause yer a dried grape of a thing, yer a raisin – (*Beat.*) I knackered it, didn't I, Ruairi? Or all of us did. It's only who we are.

Ruairi I didn't drink the money from the suit, Ma.

Millie Sure ye didn't.

Ruairi I didn't. I could've, but I didn't.

Millie It's only who we are, Ruairi.

Ruairi I never can speak in this place – I have this awful silence in me.

Millie The baby's dead, ye know? Edna's baby. (*Motioning next door.*) I've been in there at the wake. That'll be it now. I could see it in all their faces, ye know? Just like the last time.

Ruairi I have te go, Ma.

Millie Ye wanna be a comfort te me, son?

She opens her arms for him to come and hug her. He doesn't move.

Not a big man like you, hey?

He starts towards the stairs. More to herself:

Ye were a beautiful baby. Always smiling.

He turns and looks at her, then exits. Left alone she drinks from the whiskey bottle. Someone next door has begun to play the tune to the Irish folk song 'The Water is Wide' solemnly on a fiddle. Millie sings the first verse along with it.

The water is wide, I cannot cross o'er.
And neither have I
The wings to fly.
Build me a boat, that can carry two.
And both shall row,
My true love . . .

As she sings, her eyes wander to Fergal and, seeing his face covered, she breaks off abruptly. She goes to him quickly, pulling back the sheet, recoiling.

Millie Ruairi!

She tries to pull him up in the bed, shaking him.

Da. Da. Come on, Da. Da!

She begins to smack him on the back as if he were having a coughing fit. She starts to shake him violently.

Hey! Come on! Jesus, come on, come on.

She grabs the whiskey bottle and tries to force-feed him drink. Niamh enters at the door and, taking this in for a split second, runs to Millie and wrestles the bottle from her. Millie struggles and screams, so Niamh has to restrain her physically.

Off me!

Niamh Jesus.

Millie Let me help him!

Niamh He's dead, Ma.

Millie No!

Niamh Look at him. (*Holding Millie tightly now to keep her still.*) Look at him. He's dead.

Millie stops struggling, the pair of them coming to rest at last almost in an embrace. Pause.

Millie Ruairi was here –

Niamh He'll break in two over this.

Millie (*the full impact of Fergal's death hitting her suddenly*) No!

She starts to cry violently, throwing Niamh off her.

No!

Niamh Stop it, Ma.

Millie No.

Millie paces the room like an animal.

Niamh Please, Ma –

Millie No.

Niamh Ma –

Millie No. No. No.

Niamh Ma, fer God's sake –

Pause, as Millie eyes Niamh.

Millie Do you know how much death I've seen?

Beat. Niamh only looks at her.

Five sisters, two brothers, tens of tens of friends and strangers. De you know how little I've come te be moved by death? Watched yer drunken father sink, wave, drown in the river, and couldn't do a bleedin thing about it. That's my life. Standing there watchin things die and I can't do a bleedin thing about it. But *him*, he lived. That's what he did.

She collapses to a sitting position on the floor.

That's what he did.

The fiddle plays next door. She sits for some moments, numb.

Perhaps Mrs Adler's right about us, hey? All our kind should have all starved in Ireland years ago, 'cause this is not our place on God's earth. (*She scratches at the dirt floor.*) This isn't God's earth at all. It's ours. Thick with fever and filth. It's our punishment.

Niamh He's just dead, Ma. There's no God in it.

Brynjar appears in the doorway. He pauses, taking in the scene in confusion.

Brynjar Millie?

Millie Leave me.

Brynjar What's happened?

Millie Leave me!

He hovers for a moment in the doorway.

99

Niamh Why ye standin there? She needs ye.

He goes and pulls Millie tightly to him.

Millie (*struggling*) Leave me. Ye don't want me.

Brynjar (*continuing to hold her tightly*) How long since he is dead?

Millie Leave me. You don't want me. She's right –

Brynjar (*to Niamh*) Did she see him die?

Millie She's right. She's right. I can't wash this off.

Brynjar I won't leave you –

Millie She's right! She's always been cleverer than me and she's right.

Brynjar What is right?

Millie How do I wash this off? It's in us.

Brynjar What's in you?

Millie The dirt. The fever. She knew you'd go. She's cleverer than me.

Brynjar Stop it now, stop it.

Millie I can't wash it off. (*Pushing him off.*) Just leave me.

Brynjar I won't, I promise.

Millie I'll make you. Whatever you forgive me for, I'll do worse.

Brynjar I love you.

Millie You love something you think of me – some made-up thing –

Brynjar You don't believe that.

Millie It's never been me.

Brynjar I wanted something for you –

Millie Did ye have to? Did ye have te start wanting for me? Making me want along with yer? Making me believe that I was worth it? I'm only what I've always been.

Brynjar I've only wanted what you've always been.

Millie That's not true.

Brynjar You remember how I saw you? Hah? Remember the first time I saw you? You are lying on the street, drunk. Your hair is in a puddle, in a gutter. People are stepping over you. And when I help you up, you look me in the eye and you are not ashamed. You laugh. (*Beat.*) You remember?

> *Millie nods.*

I liked you already in the gutter, when you laughed. I liked you because you laughed and were not ashamed. I was a foreign man with no money and no home, barely understanding people when they speak. I felt I was the lowest man in the world and I met you, lying on the ground and *laughing*. (*Beat.*) It was not pity I felt then.

Millie I thought ye'd left me. Me an yer child.

Brynjar Where would I go? I walked out today blind with feeling, just walking and walking, and when I realised where I was standing I saw I'd walked the length of the town and back to here. Where else would I come back to? My family is here.

> *Pause. Next door the wake is becoming a party: the sound of 'The Water is Wide' in full group rendition, repeating the same two verses:*

The water is wide, I cannot cross o'er,
And neither have I the wings to fly.
Build me a boat, that can carry two,
And both shall row, my true love and I.

A ship there is, and she sails the seas.
She's laden deep, as deep can be,
But not so deep, as the love I'm in,
And I know not if, I sink or swim.

Millie And if this is all there is?

Brynjar Then this is all I am.

Millie How can I have a new life with you, Brynjar?

Pause as she looks at her father's body.

You tell me how I ever wash this off?

Niamh goes and lifts the now-full bucket of rainwater. She carries it to Fergal's side, pulls back the sheet and starts to sponge Fergal's upper body. In time the other two separate and echo her, cupping water between their hands and letting it fall onto Fergal's body. The singing next door grows louder on the last verse as more voices join, until the sound is almost a crescendo. Lights down.

SCENE FIVE: IRREVERENCE

Early hours of the next morning: Millie, Brynjar and Niamh are sat at the table, drinking the dregs of the whiskey in turn: Brynjar facing outwards with pen and paper, and Millie and Niamh facing each other. A sheet has been tightly drawn over Fergal's body. The bucket remains beside Fergal so that the now steady rhythm of water falls down, hitting dully onto the floor of the room. Next door's reverence has turned into a drunken knees-up: chatter, shouts, stomping feet, a fiddle and an accordion being heard through the wall.

Brynjar 'Dearest Father.'

Millie Dearest Daddy.

Brynjar 'Dearest Papa. For a year my letters to you have been lies. I never got to New York, Father.' (*He writes*)

Millie (*of Fergal*) The Pickled Miracle, they call him round the court. Have ye heard them say that? 'The Pickled Miracle.'

Niamh I've heard that.

Millie They'll sing fer him, when they hear. The whole court – all the courts – they'll howl.

Brynjar 'I have lived in Liverpool, in a cellar room with no window and a hole in the roof.'

Millie There'll be some drinks raised to him when the news gets round, don't ye think?

Niamh There will, Ma.

Brynjar 'I have a wife who lives by pulling apart old rope to sell. She has a son and a daughter and we will soon have a baby, who if he is a boy, I will name after you.'

A pause as he writes this down.

Millie He might've played the piano to yer once or twice. Yer da. He might've done that.

Niamh (*beat*) I dunno . . . It was probably you.

Brynjar 'This is who I am, Papa, and perhaps I am not yet the fine man you worked for me to be; but many a great man died in a hole in the ground; and while I have breath I will strive for more.'

Millie (*to Brynjar*) Ye still believe there's more?

Brynjar (*setting about writing what he has just orated*) I would not write it to my papa if it was not true.

Pause as Brynjar writes. From next door many voices sing, slowly, drunkenly, in unison:

Sing a song that the ship might sail
For all the things the sea might save,
Raise a drink for broken things
Scattered on the wave.

*They repeat this, not knowing the rest of the words,
each time one voice taking it up again, and the rest
joining in dutifully. Niamh pulls her money from her
clothes and puts it down on the table.*

Niamh (*pushing it towards Millie*) Here. Buy yerself a
new piano.

Millie (*pushing it back*) It's not my money.

Niamh (*imploring*) Ma.

*A pause. Millie eyes the money awkwardly. She accepts
it.*

Millie Thank you.

Brynjar Perhaps we should go out and walk through the
streets. The people will still be dancing. I saw thousands
of people stamping and chanting and tumbling all the
way up to the steps of the hall. Girls were dancing up
there with bright ribbons and there was trumpet music
floating in and out as the wind changed. A man was
shouting a speech about the power of the sea but no one
could hear him. They had all brought their own songs to
sing. (*He writes fervently.*)

Millie If Ruairi was here he'd be livid and cursing the lot
of them.

Niamh Perhaps he was in amongst them, dancing.

*The leak from the roof has become a steady rhythm
again. The music from next door gets louder, the
remaining revellers stamping on the floor to the
accordion.*

Millie (*picking up the bottle of whiskey; toasting*) To the Pickled Miracle.

She drinks from the bottle, then passes it on. Niamh drinks from the bottle and passes it to Brynjar.

Brynjar (*taking a drink from the bottle*) The Pickled Miracle.

Niamh (*takes the bottle*) The Pickled Miracle.

She drinks the final drops.

Brynjar There were so many people that you had to believe that it mattered, if it mattered to everybody else. I saw half the court mixed in there; laughing and dancing and straining to see – the great hall looming and the whole city shouting to be seen. (*Beat.*) They were proud. (*Beat.*) They were really proud.

The music next door gets louder, accompanied by footstamping so the building almost shakes. After a moment Millie begins to bang the empty bottle against the table in time with the music and the steady drip of rain that continues to fall against the ground. Brynjar's pen knocks against the hard surface as he resumes writing. Niamh leans back and forth on her chair, allowing it to bump against the ground, caught in the motion of this rhythm. Flies buzz.

Lights down. End.